THE MANUAL OF LEARNING STYLES

by

Peter Honey and Alan Mumford

Introduction to second edition.

The Manual of Learning Styles was first published in November 1982 and reprinted in 1984. In this second edition we have included a revised version of the questionnaire and the descriptions of the styles. A fuller explanation of these changes is given on page 84 but, in general terms, we have simplified the language and removed most of the colloquialisms.

Copyright © 1986 Peter Honey and Alan Mumford
Published and distributed by Peter Honey, Ardingly House, 10 Linden Avenue, Maidenhead, Berkshire, SL6 6HB.

ISBN 0 9508444 0 3

Printed by Printique, Maidenhead, Berkshire.

THE MANUAL OF LEARNING STYLES

Peter Honey and Alan Mumford

Contents Page

Chapter 1
The Influences on Effective Learning

The Significance of the Individual

The ideas and practices offered in this manual arose from the question we have both faced in advising on the processes of developing more effective managers. The question can be described through a common experience. Two managers, as a result of a careful analysis showing their learning needs, arrived at with their full participation and commitment, are put through the same learning experience. The learning experience has been designed with the greatest care, and both managers have the advantage of subtle counselling and tutorial help. One manager reports the experience as very useful, and demonstrates by his subsequent actions that he has indeed learned from it. The other manager is considerably less enthusiastic, perhaps even hostile; he gives no evidence subsequently that his behaviour has been changed.

The question we and others face is why, with other factors apparently common, one person learns and another does not? We aim to show that the reason for this divergence lies in the differing reaction of the individuals, explicable by their different needs for the way in which learning is offered. Their requirements are described here in shorthand as their learning styles; we show how these styles can be identified and the kind of learning behaviour which creates the style. We go on to show how this knowledge can be used to enable a better choice to be made for individuals amongst available learning opportunities.

A Definition of Learning

In our view a manager has learned something when either or both of the following descriptions apply:-

● He knows something he did not know earlier, and can show it.

● He is able to do something he was not able to do before.

The Range of Influences

The history of the development of ways of helping managers to learn how to be more effective is relatively short; perhaps forty years in the U.K. a little longer in the U.S.A. One of the constant features in that history has been the discovery of a succession of what were claimed to be uniquely appropriate and necessary aspects of the process of learning. Lectures were abandoned and replaced by case studies. Books about human relations techniques were replaced by T Groups, structured training needs analyses gave way to individual commitment to self development. The problem of ineffective learning remains, because these "solutions" dealt too exclusively with a generalised teaching method and not with differences in individual approaches to learning.

This manual is about the contribution which can be made to effective learning by an understanding and use of individual styles of learning. We are, however, clear that we are describing a contribution, one of several major aspects which must be 'right' before effective learning occurs. We are not adding another innovation and claiming that without it nothing useful will be done; we are saying that with attention to individual learning styles, much more effective learning can take place.

In order to emphasise the importance of placing learning styles in the total learning context, it is worth reminding readers of the large number of factors which influence the extent of learning.

The Manager's Job determines what kind of managerial experiences and skills are necessary for effective performance. Research, and our own experience, show considerable differences in requirements within jobs even apparently similar in title. Learning needs are best seen as specific, not general, much affected by particular organisational demands; they are also dynamic not static.

The Manager's Environment influences both the need for, and the attitudes to, learning. Many attempts to influence learning break down because parts of the environment are unhelpful or even positively hostile. The environment includes a number of relatively large scale structural factors such as the way in which organisational priorities and objectives are expressed through an organisational structure, and whether the organisation is in a steady state or is highly turbulent. The organisational climate can be felt, if not measured; "the way things are round here" can be positive or inimical to learning in general or to particular kinds of learning. When powerful people show interest through the system they favour, through the rewards they provide for effective learning and from their personal involvement, then important parts of the climate are positive.

The environmental aspects also include the smaller scale but perhaps more directly influential interventions of individuals, particularly boss and colleagues. Few bosses provide an encouraging learning environment, one in which learning needs and opportunities are consciously identified and pursued. Potentially, however, the boss has a crucial role in providing coaching or providing a personal model of effective behaviour.

Perhaps most crucial of all is the influence of structure, climate and the personal interactions of boss and colleagues in providing rewards to the manager for his attempts to learn. It is our strong belief that managerial behaviour is much affected by the expectations of consequences; both willingness to learn and what is learned are substantially influenced by the consequences anticipated by the potential learner.

The Analysis of Learning Needs

Even if the environment is encouraging it is obvious that effective learning will only take place if learning needs have been properly identified. What we have to say about the benefits of choosing learning opportunities related to individual learning styles could still be rendered useless if we were trying to match styles and opportunities in pursuit of what were, in fact, inappropriate needs. Whether through self analysis, performance appraisal, multi-person analyses (e.g. through the Repertory Grid), the analysis must in the end meet the basic requirements of being directed at the performance criteria in the job, and be incorporated into the individual's concept of himself as a manager.

The Providers of Learning Opportunities

We are gradually developing a better understanding of the roles of boss and colleagues in providing learning opportunities. As coaches, mentors and models, they provide occasional, but powerful, experiences, in the normal work environment. Off the job, tutors (or facilitators as some now call themselves) more obviously are in business to provide opportunities. In both areas there is scope for major improvement, particularly in providing opportunities focussed on the needs of the recipient rather than on the interests of the provider. Our work on learning styles provides an additional factor because, as we show later, it is now possible to match the styles of learners and the providers of learning (See Chapter 6). Too often the providers of learning are offering something in a way which is not congruent with the way in which at least some of their subordinates or students, will learn effectively. Equally, many advisers on management development have not thought about the compatibility of a course of learning experience with learning style.

The Nature of Learning

We have already expressed our emphasis on learning as a process which can best be based on the provision of consequences that are rewarding. We are not going to examine here the processes of stimulus, response, feedback, reward and reinforcement. It is, however, desirable that we should identify the theoretical background which is particularly crucial to learning styles, and to acknowledge our debt to Kolb, whose theory of learning and identification of learning styles was the origin of successively our interest, our dissatisfaction and our development work.

Kolb's was a theory explicity based on a view of learning as a series of experiences with cognitive additions rather than as a series of pure cognitive processes. He saw learning as a circular process in which Concrete Experience is followed by Reflection and Observation; this in turn leads to the formulation of Abstract Concepts and Generalisations, the implications of which are tested in new situations through Active Experimentation. While his theory described an integrated process, in which all stages have to be completed, he then moved on to say that people were rarely fully effective in all stages. He produced variants of his main stages and by combining various parts of the four stages, identified four main styles of learner, and used a Learning Style Inventory to establish an individual's relative emphasis on each of the four styles.

While we found the circular learning pattern acceptable, we grew less happy with the content and results of the Learning Style Inventory. The L.S.I. is based on responses to 36 words (not sentences) which do not describe managerial activities; as a basis for the attribution of styles we found them less persuasive both to us and to managers. Nor did we find his descriptions of the styles as Converger, Diverger, Assimilator, Accommodator, either congruent with our own experiences, or meaningful to many of the managers with whom we dealt.

Since our concern was not to put managers into types, but to find a way of improving the effectiveness of learning, we wanted to have a tool which was both more readily acceptable to managers and which would provide us with a base from which we could more credibly develop ways of providing guidance on individual learning styles and associated learning behaviour. We had already therefore, developed the main outline of our approach before reading the academic criticisms of Kolb by Freedman and Stumpf.

Our debt to Kolb remains; we have accepted the idea of a four stage process of learning, and we have developed a view of four main styles of learning which appear to have much in common, at the general level, with Kolb. We have diverged in two major ways however. Firstly, we have built our views of the learning styles, and the questionnaire, around recognisable statements of managerial behaviour. This in turn has meant that our descriptions of learning styles are both more detailed than, and differ from their apparent Kolb equivalents.

Secondly, our approach has been dominated by the view that the answers secured from the questionnaires are a starting point not a finishing point. It might be the case that Freedman and Stumpf could have as much academic criticism to offer on our process as they did of Kolb. (Although our work has been refined and tested over ten years). Our main concern, however, has not been to produce something that is academically respectable, but to produce something which will give detailed practical guidance to those who are trying to develop their abilities, and to those who are trying to help them.

We have not incorporated in our work any of the insights offered by the work done by Margerison and Lewis, based on the Myers Briggs questionnaire; this is in turn based on Jungian psychology. While we find this work of interest, our own strong preference is to concentrate on observable behaviour rather than on the psychological basis for that behaviour. We believe it more useful to identify how behaviour can be modified, rather than to explain the background to the behaviour.

The Importance of Knowing How You Learn

This is a practical work manual, not a research study. We believe that knowledge of your own learning style, or of the styles of others, will help secure more effective learning, if the knowledge is used rather than merely recorded. In later chapters we describe how this can be done; perhaps the most significant uses are:-

- Increased awareness of learning activities which are congruent or incongruent with the dominant learning style of the individual.

- A better choice among those activities, leading to more effective and more economical learning provision. Avoidance of inappropriate learning experiences is both good in itself and less likely to lead to the Shakespeare effect, where inappropriate early experiences put young people off for life.

- An identification of areas in which an individual's less effective learning processes can be improved.

- Development of ways in which specific learning skills can be improved, e.g. planning learning goals or analysing successful performers.

Throughout this manual we have used 'he' not 'she'. By far the majority of results we have are for men. We show on page 79 the norms we have for women which show very marginal differences, of little significance. This is one of several areas in which we hope that those readers who join the L.S.Q. Club (See Page 82) will provide us with relevant information, so that we can, for example, compare male/female scores in the same functions.

Chapter 2

The Learning Styles Questionnaire

This chapter contains the Learning Styles Questionnaire (L.S.Q.), descriptions of the four learning styles it probes, the method of scoring the questionnaire and some advice on how to interpret the results.

The questionnaire has a total of 80 items which people are asked to tick or cross to indicate whether, on balance, they agree or disagree. The vast majority of items are behavioural, i.e. they describe an action that someone might or might not be seen to take. Occasionally an item probes a preference or belief rather than a manifest behaviour. In common with all questionnaires of this type, the L.S.Q. is designed to discover *general* trends or tendencies running through a person's behaviour and does not place undue significance on any of the items.

Here then, is the L.S.Q. together with the instructions on how to complete it. We have found that the few lines of introduction/instructions give people sufficient information prior to completing the questionnaire. Discussion of the learning styles themselves is best postponed until the whole questionnaire has been completed. (See Chapter 6 for suggestions on how to proceed with discussion).

THE LEARNING STYLES QUESTIONNAIRE

This questionnaire is designed to find out your preferred learning style(s). Over the years you have probably developed learning 'habits' that help you benefit more from some experiences than from others. Since you are probably unaware of this, this questionnaire will help you pinpoint your learning preferences so that you are in a better position to select learning experiences that suit your style.

There is no time limit to this questionnaire. It will probably take you 10-15 minutes. The accuracy of the results depends on how honest you can be. There are no right or wrong answers. If you agree more than you disagree with a statement put a tick by it (✓). If you disagree more than you agree put a cross by it (✗). Be sure to mark each item with either a tick or cross.

- ☐ 1. I have strong beliefs about what is right and wrong, good and bad.
- ☐ 2. I often act without considering the possible consequences.
- ☐ 3. I tend to solve problems using a step-by-step approach.

☐ 4. I believe that formal procedures and policies restrict people.

☐ 5. I have a reputation for saying what I think, simply and directly.

☐ 6. I often find that actions based on feelings are as sound as those based on careful thought and analysis.

☐ 7. I like the sort of work where I have time for thorough preparation and implementation.

☐ 8. I regularly question people about their basic assumptions.

☐ 9. What matters most is whether something works in practice.

☐ 10. I actively seek out new experiences.

☐ 11. When I hear about a new idea or approach I immediately start working out how to apply it in practice.

☐ 12. I am keen on self discipline such as watching my diet, taking regular exercise, sticking to a fixed routine, etc.

☐ 13. I take pride in doing a thorough job.

☐ 14. I get on best with logical, analytical people and less well with spontaneous, 'irrational' people.

☐ 15. I take care over the interpretation of data available to me and avoid jumping to conclusions.

☐ 16. I like to reach a decision carefully after weighing up many alternatives.

☐ 17. I'm attracted more to novel, unusual ideas than to practical ones.

☐ 18. I don't like disorganised things and prefer to fit things into a coherent pattern.

☐ 19. I accept and stick to laid down procedures and policies so long as I regard them as an efficient way of getting the job done.

☐ 20. I like to relate my actions to a general principle.

☐ 21. In discussions I like to get straight to the point.

☐ 22. I tend to have distant, rather formal relationships with people at work

☐ 23. I thrive on the challenge of tackling something new and different.

☐ 24. I enjoy fun-loving, spontaneous people.

☐ 25. I pay meticulous attention to detail before coming to a conclusion.

☐ 26. I find it difficult to produce ideas on impulse.

☐ 27. I believe in coming to the point immediately.

☐ 28. I am careful not to jump to conclusions too quickly.

☐ 29. I prefer to have as many sources of information as possible - the more data to think over the better.

☐ 30. Flippant people who don't take things seriously enough usually irritate me.

☐ 31. I listen to other people's points of view before putting my own forward.

☐ 32. I tend to be open about how I'm feeling.

☐ 33. In discussions I enjoy watching the manoeuverings of the other participants.

☐ 34. I prefer to respond to events on a spontaneous, flexible basis rather than plan things out in advance.

☐ 35. I tend to be attracted to techniques such as network analysis, flow charts, branching programmes, contingency planning, etc.

☐ 36. It worries me if I have to rush out a piece of work to meet a tight deadline.

☐ 37. I tend to judge people's ideas on their practical merits.

☐ 38. Quiet, thoughtful people tend to make me feel uneasy.

☐ 39. I often get irritated by people who want to rush things.

☐ 40. It is more important to enjoy the present moment than to think about the past or future.

☐ 41. I think that decisions based on a thorough analysis of all the information are sounder than those based on intuition.

☐ 42. I tend to be a perfectionist.

☐ 43. In discussions I usually produce lots of spontaneous ideas.

☐ 44. In meetings I put forward practical realistic ideas.

☐ 45. More often than not, rules are there to be broken.

☐ 46. I prefer to stand back from a situation and consider all the perspectives.

☐ 47. I can often see inconsistencies and weaknesses in other people's arguments.

☐ 48. On balance I talk more than I listen.

☐ 49. I can often see better, more practical ways to get things done.

☐ 50. I think written reports should be short and to the point.

☐ 51. I believe that rational, logical thinking should win the day.

☐ 52. I tend to discuss specific things with people rather than engaging in social discussion.

☐ 53. I like people who approach things realistically rather than theoretically.

☐ 54. In discussions I get impatient with irrelevancies and digressions.

☐ 55. If I have a report to write I tend to produce lots of drafts before settling on the final version.

☐ 56. I am keen to try things out to see if they work in practice.

☐ 57. I am keen to reach answers via a logical approach.

☐ 58. I enjoy being the one that talks a lot.

☐ 59. In discussions I often find I am the realist, keeping people to the point and avoiding wild speculations.

☐ 60. I like to ponder many alternatives before making up my mind.

☐ 61. In discussions with people I often find I am the most dispassionate and objective.

☐ 62. In discussions I'm more likely to adopt a 'low profile' than to take the lead and do most of the talking.

☐ 63. I like to be able to relate current actions to a longer term picture.

☐ 64. When things go wrong I am happy to shrug it off and 'put it down to experience'.

☐ 65. I tend to reject wild, spontaneous ideas as being impractical.

☐ 66. It's best to think carefully before taking action.

☐ 67. On balance I do the listening rather than the talking.

☐ 68. I tend to be tough on people who find it difficult to adopt a logical approach.

☐ 69. Most times I believe the end justifies the means.

☐ 70. I don't mind hurting people's feelings so long as the job gets done.

☐ 71. I find the formality of having specific objectives and plans stifling.

☐ 72. I'm usually one of the people who puts life into a party.

☐ 73. I do whatever is expedient to get the job done.

☐ 74. I quickly get bored with methodical, detailed work.

☐ 75. I am keen on exploring the basic assumptions, principles and theories underpinning things and events.

☐ 76. I'm always interested to find out what people think.

☐ 77. I like meetings to be run on methodical lines, sticking to laid down agenda, etc.

☐ 78. I steer clear of subjective or ambiguous topics.

☐ 79. I enjoy the drama and excitement of a crisis situation.

☐ 80. People often find me insensitive to their feelings.

Descriptions of the Learning Styles

The L.S.Q. is designed to probe the relative strengths of four different learning styles. This section gives a paragraph summarising each of the styles and 'unscrambles' the questionnaire by revealing which items go with which style (there are 20 questionnaire items for each style).

The names given to the four styles are, in no order of importance, Activist, Reflector, Theorist, Pragmatist. Here is a description of each:-

Activists
Activists involve themselves fully and without bias in new experiences. They enjoy the here and now and are happy to be dominated by immediate experiences. They are open-minded, not sceptical, and this tends to make them enthusiastic about anything new. Their philosophy is: 'I'll try anything once'. They tend to act first and consider the consequences afterwards. Their days are filled with activity. They tackle problems by brainstorming. As soon as the excitement from one activity has died down they are busy looking for the next. They tend to thrive on the challenge of new experiences but are bored with implementation and longer term consolidation. They are gregarious people constantly involving themselves with others but, in doing so, they seek to centre all activities around themselves.

Activist questionnaire items:-

2. I often act without considering the possible consequences.

4. I believe that formal procedures and policies restrict people.

6. I often find that actions based on feelings are as sound as those based on careful thought and analysis.

10. I actively seek out new experiences.

17. I'm attracted more to novel, unusual ideas than to practical ones.

23. I thrive on the challenge of tackling something new and different

24. I enjoy fun-loving, spontaneous people.

32. I tend to be open about how I'm feeling.

34. I prefer to respond to events on a spontaneous, flexible basis rather than plan things out in advance.

38. Quiet, thoughtful people tend to make me feel uneasy.

40. It is more important to enjoy the present moment than to think about the past or future.

43. In discussions I usually produce lots of spontaneous ideas.

45. More often than not, rules are there to be broken.

48. On balance I talk more than I listen.

58. I enjoy being the one that talks a lot.

64. When things go wrong I am happy to shrug it off and 'put it down to experience'.

71. I find the formality of having specific objectives and plans stifling.

72. I'm usually one of the people who puts life into a party.

74. I quickly get bored with methodical, detailed work.

79. I enjoy the drama and excitement of a crisis situation.

Reflectors
Reflectors like to stand back to ponder experiences and observe them from many different perspectives. They collect data, both first hand and from others, and prefer to think about it thoroughly before coming to any conclusion. The thorough collection and analysis of data about experiences and events is what counts so they tend to postpone reaching definitive conclusions for as long as possible. Their philosophy is to be cautious. They are thoughtful people who like to consider all possible angles and implications before making a move. They prefer to take a back seat in meetings and discussions. They enjoy observing other people in action. They listen to others and get the drift of the discussion before making their own points. They tend to adopt a low profile and have a slightly distant, tolerant

unruffled air about them. When they act it is part of a wide picture which includes the past as well as the present and others' observations as well as their own.

Reflector questionaire items:-

7. I like the sort of work where I have time for thorough preparation and implementation.
13. I take pride in doing a thorough job.
15. I take care over the interpretation of data available to me and avoid jumping to conclusions.
16. I like to reach a decision carefully after weighing up many alternatives.
25. I pay meticulous attention to detail before coming to a conclusion.
28. I am careful not to jump to conclusions too quickly.
29. I prefer to have as many sources of information as possible - the more data to think over the better.
31. I listen to other people's points of view before putting my own forward.
33. In discussions I enjoy watching the manoeuvrings of the other participants.
36. It worries me if I have to rush out a piece of work to meet a tight deadline.
39. I often get irritated by people who want to rush things.
41. I think that decisions based on a thorough analysis of all the information are sounder than those based on intuition.
46. I prefer to stand back from a situation and consider all the perspectives.
52. I tend to discuss specific things with people rather than engaging in social discussion.
55. If I have a report to write I tend to produce lots of drafts before settling on the final version.
60. I like to ponder many alternatives before making up my mind.
62. In discussions I'm more likely to adopt a 'low profile' than to take the lead and do most of the talking.

66. It's best to think carefully before taking action.

67. On balance I do the listening rather than the talking.

76. I'm always interested to find out what people think.

Theorists

Theorists adapt and integrate observations into complex but logically sound theories. They think problems through in a vertical, step by step logical way. They assimilate disparate facts into coherent theories. They tend to be perfectionists who won't rest easy until things are tidy and fit into a rational scheme. They like to analyse and synthesise. They are keen on basic assumptions, principles, theories models and systems thinking. Their philosophy prizes rationality and logic. 'If it's logical it's good'. Questions they frequently ask are: "Does it make sense?" "How does this fit with that?" "What are the basic assumptions?" They tend to be detached, analytical and dedicated to rational objectivity rather than anything subjective or ambiguous. Their approach to problems is consistently logical. This is their 'mental set' and they rigidly reject anything that doesn't fit with it. They prefer to maximise certainty and feel uncomfortable with subjective judgements, lateral thinking and anything flippant.

Theorist questionnaire items:-

1. I have strong beliefs about what is right and wrong, good and bad.

3. I tend to solve problems using a step-by-step approach.

8. I regularly question people about their basic assumptions.

12. I am keen on self discipline such as watching my diet, taking regular exercise, sticking to a fixed routine, etc.

14. I get on best with logical, analytical people and less well with spontaneous, 'irrational' people.

18. I don't like disorganised things and prefer to fit things into a coherent pattern.

20. I like to relate my actions to a general principle.

22. I tend to have distant, rather formal relationships with people at work.

26. I find it difficult to produce ideas on impulse.

30. Flippant people who don't take things seriously enough usually irritate me.

42. I tend to be a perfectionist.

47. I can often see inconsistencies and weaknesses in other people's arguments.

51. I believe that rational, logical thinking should win the day.

57. I am keen to reach answers via a logical approach.

61. In discussions with people I often find I am the most dispassionate and objective.

63. I like to be able to relate current actions to a longer term bigger picture.

68. I tend to be tough on people who find it difficult to adopt a logical approach.

75. I am keen on exploring the basic assumptions, principles and theories underpinning things and events.

77. I like meetings to be run on methodical lines, sticking to laid down agenda, etc.

78. I steer clear of subjective or ambiguous topics.

Pragmatists
Pragmatists are keen on trying out ideas, theories and techniques to see if they work in practice. They positively search out new ideas and take the first opportunity to experiment with applications. They are the sort of people who return from management courses brimming with new ideas that they want to try out in practice. They like to get on with things and act quickly and confidently on ideas that attract them. They tend to be impatient with ruminating and open-ended discussions. They are essentialy practical, down to earth people who like making practical decisions and solving problems. They respond to problems and opportunities 'as a challenge'. Their philosophy is: 'There is always a better way' and 'If it *works* it's good'.

Pragmatist questionnaire items:-

5. I have a reputation for saying what I think, simply and directly.

9. What matters most is whether something works in practice.

11. When I hear about a new idea or approach I immediately start working out how to apply it in practice.

19. I accept and stick to laid down procedures and policies so long as I regard them as an efficient way of getting the job done.

21. In discussions I like to get straight to the point.

27. I believe in coming to the point immediately.

35. I tend to be attracted to techniques such as network analysis, flow charts, branching programmes, contingency planning, etc.

37. I tend to judge people's ideas on their practical merits.

44. In meetings I put forward practical realistic ideas.

49. I can often see better, more practical ways to get things done.

50. I think written reports should be short and to the point.

53. I like people who approach things realistically rather than theoretically.

54. In discussions I get impatient with irrelevancies and digressions.

56. I am keen to try things out to see if they work in practice.

59. In discussions I often find I am the realist, keeping people to the point and avoiding wild speculations.

65. I tend to reject wild, spontaneous ideas as being impractical.

69. Most times I believe the end justifies the means.

70. I don't mind hurting people's feelings so long as the job gets done.

73. I do whatever is expedient to get the job done.

80. People often find me insensitive to their feelings.

Scoring and Interpreting the L.S.Q.

The L.S.Q. is scored by awarding one point for each ticked item. There are no points for crossed items.

Simply indicate on the lists below which items were ticked.

2	7	1	5
4	13	3	9
6	15	8	11
10	16	12	19
17	25	14	21
23	28	18	27
24	29	20	35
32	31	22	37
34	33	26	44
38	36	30	49
40	39	42	50
43	41	47	53
45	46	51	54
48	52	57	56
58	55	61	59
64	60	63	65
71	62	68	69
72	66	75	70
74	67	77	73
79	76	78	80

Totals

Activist *Reflector* *Theorist* *Pragmatist*

Since the maximum total possible for each style is twenty at first sight, it would appear that the highest of the four scores indicates the predominant learning style. However, this is not necessarily so. Before drawing a conclusion the raw scores need to be viewed in the context of the score patterns that emerge from the L.S.Q. norms. The final chapter of this manual gives norms for various groups of people but to illustrate how to use them to arrive at a conclusion we will use the general norms given in Chapter 7 on Page 75. For those unfamiliar with the concept of norms we should explain that it is a way of expressing the scores given by different groups of people to form a useful basis of comparison. The scores obtained by any group are analysed to see what score ranges have been obtained by:-

● The top 10% of people in the group.

● The next 20% of people in the group.

● The middle 40% of people in the group.

● The next 20% of people in the group.

● The bottom 10% of people in the group.

Let us suppose the raw scores for an individual are Activist 11, Reflector 11, Theorist 11, Pragmatist 11. We have chosen these scores because they admirably illustrate the importance of using the norms to reach an interpretation rather than jumping to a conclusion based on the raw scores alone. If you plot the raw scores onto a L.S.Q. profile based on the general norms the following picture emerges:-

L.S.Q. Profile Based on General Norms for 1302 People (Chapter 7 Page 75)

Activist	Reflector	Theorist	Pragmatist	
20	20	20	20	
19		19		
18			19	
17	19	18		Very strong preference
16			18	
15		17		
14				
13	18	16	17	
12	17	15	16	
	16			Strong preference
(11)	15	14	15	
10	14	13	14	
9	13	12	13	Moderate preference
8				
7	12	(11)	12	
6	(11)	10	(11)	
5	10	9	10	Low preference
4	9	8	9	
3	8	7	8	
	7	6	7	
	6	5	6	
2	5	4	5	
	4	3	4	Very low preference
1	3	2	3	
	2	1	2	
0	1		1	
	0	0	0	

According to the norms therefore, the conclusion for this individual is that Activist predominates with moderate Theorist and low preference for Reflector and Pragmatist. In effect, therefore, the norms are weighting the raw scores in different ways and this can make a substantial difference to the interpretation of L.S.Q. results. Clearly the norms for different occupational groups vary (sometimes considerably – for example, contrast the norms for salesmen on Page 76 with those for finance managers on Page 78) and it is therefore important to use the most appropriate norms, i.e. for groups that most closely match the person or people taking the L.S.Q.

L.S.Q. profiles with clear distinctions between high and low preferences are obviously the most straightforward to interpret. Profiles that put all four scores in virtually a straight horizontal line are more difficult to decipher. If the horizontal line shows a moderate or strong preference for all four styles it is likely that the person is an 'all-rounder' using, and equally at home with, each learning style. The all-rounder is likely to be better at adapting to and benefiting from a wide range of learning experiences. If however, the horizontal line shows a low preference for all four learning styles it suggests that the person has been too selective in awarding ticks to the questionnaire items or that he or she has an unusually low interest in learning. As a rough guide, if there is no preference for any style and the four raw scores total less than say 25, the chances are that an abnormally high number of questionnaire items have been crossed making the validity of the responses questionable. In our experience this rarely happens. Our statistics show (see Page 81) that the mean for the four scores combined is 48.

A useful pictorial way of showing a person's L.S.Q. result is to plot the four scores gained onto the arms of a cross, join them up to make a diamond and compare its shape with the appropriate norms. Here are a number of examples giving typical results together with a few interpretative notes.

Case 1

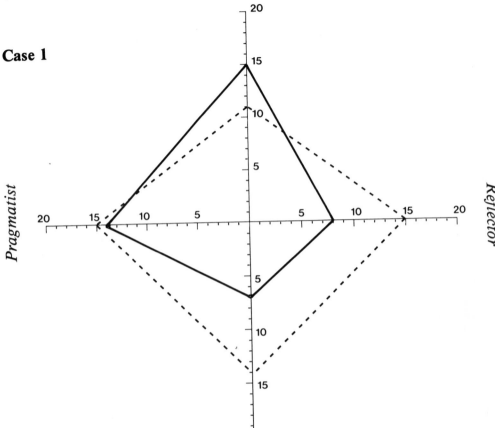

Activist

Pragmatist

Reflector

Theorist

The dotted line in this diagram is plotted from the General Norms on Page 75 to show the scores gained by the highest 30% of people. In other words, any score which coincides with or exceeds the dotted line indicates a strong preference. In this case the Activist score of 15 is the only one to go outside the dotted line and this immediately indicates a very strong preference for the Activist style. The Pragmatist score of 14 nearly coincides with the dotted line and therefore emerges as a moderate preference. Both the Reflector and Theorist scores of 8 and 7 respectively are well inside the dotted line showing a low preference for those styles.

Of course the dotted line can be varied, thus changing the basis of comparison and the interpretation, depending on which norms it is drawn from. It can also be plotted to represent the mean scores in each case rather than cutting in, as we do in this example, to show the scores gained by the highest scoring 30%.

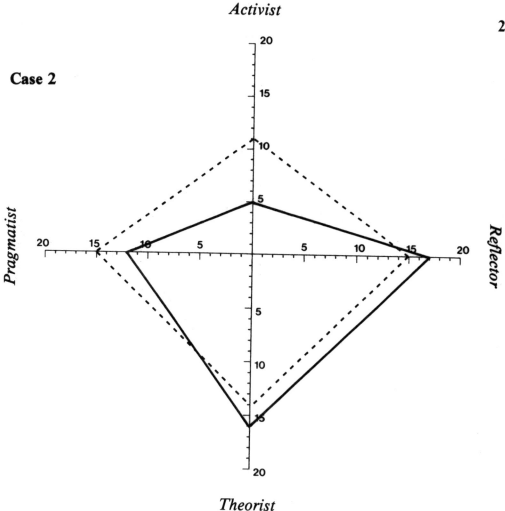

Case 2

This example is based on scoring of Activist 5, Reflector 17, Theorist 16, Pragmatist 12. It is immediately obvious that this shows a strong preference for the Theorist and Reflector styles with a moderate Pragmatist and low Activist. This is an example of an L.S.Q. profile which occurs quite frequently, particularly amongst analytical people such as scientists or accountants.

Case 3

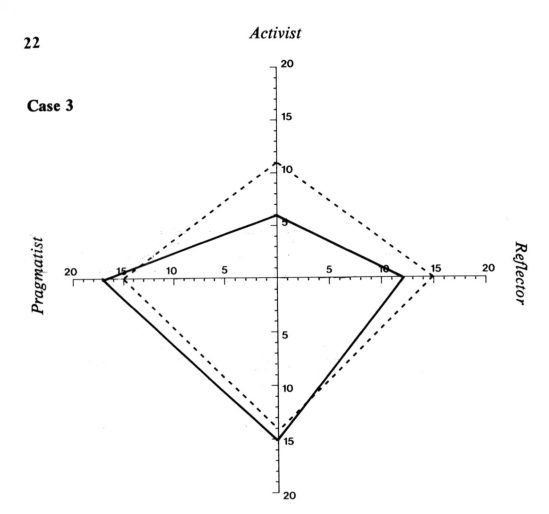

This example is based on scores of Activist 6, Reflector 12, Theorist 15, Pragmatist 17. Again it shows a combination that we have often found with a strong preference for the Pragmatist and Theorist styles and a moderate to low preference for Reflector and Activist. We have found this result to be especially typical of production managers and others in work that is closely associated with tangible, practical aspects.

Case 4

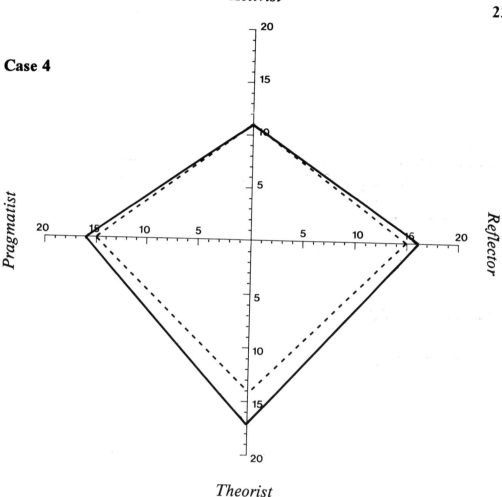

Finally, here is an example based on scores of Activist 11, Reflector 16, Theorist 17, Pragmatist 16. This shows a strong preference for all four styles and probably indicates that the person is something of an 'all-rounder'. In subsequent chapters we will have more to say about this sort of L.S.Q. result and the possibility of helping people to increase their learning style repertoire in order to act closer to this combination of styles.

As we said in the previous chapter, the identification of learning styles is only the beginning. The remainder of the chapters in this manual give guidance on how to use the information resulting from the L.S.Q. to aid more effective learning.

Introduction

We have shown in the previous chapter that there are differences in the predominant learning styles of individuals. We now go on to show that various learning activities can be assessed in terms of their relationship to learning styles. For the purpose of this manual, we are assuming that the learning needs of the individual have been properly assessed and that the individual is committed to trying to meet them. Similarly, we are assuming that the learning activity, whether on or off the job, has been properly designed according to the best principles so that, seen purely as a learning activity, it is fully efficient. (The work of Don Binsted and his colleagues deals very well with this aspect). Our concern here is to establish the difference between a learning activity which is efficient, and one which is effective for a particular individual.

The Relationship of Styles and Learning Activities

Just as some individuals are heavily dominated by one learning style, or are particularly weak in one style, so some learning activities are dominated by explicit or implicit assumptions about learning styles. The activity may be so geared to a particular style of learning as to cause a mismatch with any participant whose own major preferences are different. For example, major post experience programmes at the Business Schools tend to emphasise rationality, logic and system – values which are sought by Theorists. Some interactive skills programmes require people to learn largely through analytical reflection on experiences on the course, a process well suited to Reflectors. Generally courses reflect the learning styles of course runners not the learners; we deal with this issue in Chapter 6.

Of course just as there are individuals whose learning styles are widely spread, so there are learning activities which contain opportunities to learn in different styles. An example of this would be an interviewing course which involves role plays. A strongly Activist learner will enjoy actually playing roles; if, as is likely, he is a low Reflector, he may not learn much from that and is likely to be uncomfortable and ineffective when asked to observe others performing. Our concern then becomes to establish how learners can be helped to cope with those aspects which are foreign to their preferred learning style.

In this chapter we look first at the kind of activities which are more, or less, congruent with each of the four styles. This gives help in some situations where an individual's learning needs have been determined and we are trying to think of activities which might meet those needs.

Then we turn the coin round the other way, to look at the circumstances where someone may have received details of a learning activity and is trying to assess for himself, or for others, the kind of learner for whom it might be appropriate.

Choosing Activities Related to Styles

The activities which are most congruent with each of the styles are set out in the following lists. The lists are intended first to help guide people positively towards learning activities which they ought to find sympathetic. The learner may find that he can undertake the activities more consciously and more effectively or may find that he is missing out on some activities which ought, from his basic style, to be attractive to him.

The lists also identify activities which are much less compatible with a dominant style. In some cases the information may be used negatively – "don't try this" – but in other cases it may be possible to make the activity more acceptable despite its apparent incompatability.

Detail on the ways in which these lists can be used follows in later chapters.

Activists
Activists learn best from activities where:-

● There are *new* experiences/problems/opportunities from which to learn.

● They can engross themselves in short 'here and now' activities such as business games, competitive teamwork tasks, role-playing exercises.

● There is excitement/drama/crisis and things chop and change with a range of diverse activities to tackle.

● They have a lot of the limelight/high visibility, i.e. they can 'chair' meetings, lead discussions, give presentations.

● They are allowed to generate ideas without constraints of policy or structure or feasibility.

● They are thrown in at the deep end with a task they think is difficult, i.e. when set a challenge with inadequate resources and adverse conditions.

● They are involved with other people, i.e. bouncing ideas off them, solving problems as part of a team.

● It is appropriate to 'have a go'.

Activists learn least from, and may react against, activities where:-

● Learning involves a passive role, i.e. listening to lectures, monologues, explanations, statements of how things should be done, reading, watching.

● They are asked to stand back and not be involved.

● They are required to assimilate, analyse and interpret lots of 'messy' data.

● They are required to engage in solitary work, i.e. reading, writing, thinking on their own.

● They are asked to assess beforehand what they will learn, and to appraise afterwards what they have learned.

● They are offered statements they see as 'theoretical', i.e. explanation of cause or background.

● They are asked to repeat essentially the same activity over and over again, i.e. when practising.

● They have precise instructions to follow with little room for manouevre.

● They are asked to do a thorough job, i.e. attend to detail, tie up loose ends, dot the i's, cross t's.

Reflectors
Reflectors learn best from activities where:-

● They are allowed or encouraged to watch/think/chew over activities.

● They are able to stand back from events and listen/observe, i.e. observing a group at work, taking a back seat in a meeting, watching a film or video.

● They are allowed to think before acting, to assimilate before commenting, i.e. time to prepare, a chance to read in advance a brief giving background data.

● They can carry out some painstaking research, i.e. investigate, assemble information, probe to get to the bottom of things.

● They have the opportunity to review what has happened, what they have learned.

● They are asked to produce carefully considered analyses and reports.

● They are helped to exchange views with other people without danger, i.e. by prior agreement, within a structured learning experience.

● They can reach a decision in their own time without pressure and tight deadlines.

Reflectors learn least from, and may react against, activities where:-

- They are 'forced' into the limelight, i.e. to act as leader/chairman, to role-play in front of on-lookers.
- They are involved in situations which require action without planning.
- They are pitched into doing something without warning, i.e. to produce an instant reaction, to produce an off-the-top-of-the-head idea.
- They are given insufficient data on which to base a conclusion.
- They are given cut and dried instructions of how things should be done.
- They are worried by time pressures or rushed from one activity to another.
- In the interests of expediency they have to make short cuts or do a superficial job.

Theorists
Theorists learn best from activities where:-

- What is being offered is part of a system, model, concept, theory.
- They have time to explore methodically the associations and inter-relationships between ideas, events and situations.
- They have the chance to question and probe the basic methodology, assumptions or logic behind something, i.e. by taking part in a question and answer session, by checking a paper for inconsistencies.
- They are intellectually stretched, i.e. by analysing a complex situation, being tested in a tutorial session, by teaching high calibre people who ask searching questions.
- They are in structured situations with a clear purpose.
- They can listen to or read about ideas and concepts that emphasise rationality or logic and are well argued/elegant/watertight.
- They can analyse and then generalise the reasons for success or failure.
- They are offered interesting ideas and concepts even though they are not immediately relevant.
- They are required to understand and participate in complex situations.

Theorists learn least from, and may react against, activities where:-

- They are pitchforked into doing something without a context or apparent purpose.

- They have to participate in situations emphasising emotions and feelings.
- They are involved in unstructured activities where ambiguity and uncertainty are high, i.e. with open-ended problems, on sensitivity training.
- They are asked to act or decide without a basis in policy, principle or concept.
- They are faced with a hotchpotch of alternative/contradictory techniques/ methods without exploring any in depth, i.e. as on a 'once over lightly' course.
- They doubt that the subject matter is methodologically sound, i.e. where questionnaires haven't been validated, where there aren't any statistics to support an argument.
- They find the subject matter platitudinous, shallow or gimmicky.
- They feel themselves out of tune with other participants, i.e. when with lots of Activists or people of lower intellectual calibre.

Pragmatists
Pragmatists learn best from activities where:-

- There is an obvious link between the subject matter and a problem or opportunity on the job.
- They are shown techniques for doing things with obvious practical advantages, i.e. how to save time, how to make a good first impression, how to deal with awkward people.
- They have the chance to try out and practice techniques with coaching/ feedback from a credible expert, i.e. someone who is successful and can do the techniques themselves.
- They are exposed to a model they can emulate, i.e. a respected boss, a demonstration from someone with a proven track record, lots of examples/ anecdotes, a film showing how its done.
- They are given techniques currently applicable to their own job.
- They are given immediate opportunities to implement what they have learned.
- There is a high face validity in the learning activity, i.e. a good simulation, 'real' problems.
- They can concentrate on practical issues, i.e. drawing up action plans with an obvious end product, suggesting short cuts, giving tips.

Pragmatists learn least from, and may react against, activities where:-

● The learning is not related to an immediate need they recognise/they cannot see, an immediate relevance/practical benefit.

● Organisers of the learning, or the event itself, seems distant from reality, i.e. 'ivory towered', all theory and general principles, pure 'chalk and talk'.

● There is no practice or clear guidelines on how to do it.

● They feel that people are going round in circles and not getting anywhere fast enough.

● There are political, managerial or personal obstacles to implementation.

● There is no apparent reward from the learning activity, i.e. more sales, shorter meetings, higher bonus, promotion.

Analysis of Learning Activities
Our activity lists have given indications of the kind of learning processes which will be more, or less, successful with particular learning styles. The lists are focussed outwards from the learner; they specify the kinds of activity which will be more likely to help a learner with a particular style, and which he should seek. However, many people may have to make a choice in the reverse situation, when the first problem is to assess a particular learning opportunity (usually a course) and see what kind of learning processes are involved. In this section we turn our attention to some examples of learning opportunities and test them to see what is said explicitly, or implied, which will help determine their likely congruence with one or more learning styles. What we say is our interpretation; course brochures do not identify the relationship between what they offer and learning styles.

As we have already said, some learning opportunities involve activities appropriate to more than one style; a learner may in those cases benefit from those aspects which he finds congruent but be turned off by processes which he dislikes. In contrast, some learning opportunities are so heavily dominated by one process that the likelihood is that only those learners with a largely congruent style will learn anything.

The cases given below are illustrative of the approach we recommend, and are not a comprehensive survey of all possible learning opportunities. Our intention is to illustrate in sufficient depth and with a sufficient range of examples so that readers can pick up and use the approach themselves.

The cases about courses are anonymous in the sense that we do not quote the institutions involved. They are, however, real; all quotations are taken from descriptive material about an existing course. Our comments presume that the descriptions are a close approximation to the reality of the courses as designed by faculty and experienced by course members. We comment later on how these descriptions can be further examined to test the validity of the conclusions reached through this initial process.

A Major Post Experience Management Course
The brochure says that:-
"The programme has four major objectives around which the design has been formulated. It aims to:-

● Improve the manager's understanding of the economic, technical and social changes taking place in the environment and their implications for a company's operations.

● Increase the manager's capacity to analyse and resolve the important policy questions which face organisations in both the short and longer term.

● Improve knowledge and understanding of developments in the general and functional management processes which provide the necessary framework for managing in the face of change.

● Challenge the manager to understand and then to reinforce or modify the attitudes which influence his or her behaviour in the complex multinational business settings of today."

The brochure also gives the following information about teaching methods. (*Note,* more than incidentally, that it talks about teaching methods, not learning methods).

The brochure says that:-

"Teaching Methods
Teaching methods vary since different subjects lend themselves to varying forms of presentation. Thus, whilst lectures can be used to present facts, or highlight general background information, case discussions put the necessity for creative analysis more forcibly on to participants, guided in their analysis and discussion by the faculty. In addition, seminars, small group discussions, projects and group presentations all play a role in the programme. Groups are also used as an individual's resource for projects and as a source of feedback on his own attitudes and behaviour.

Outside the classroom or seminar room, a substantial volume of reading is necessary to supplement and prepare for class sessions, and a great deal of valuable informal discussion with faculty, with other participants or with visiting speakers, takes place. The School possesses a first-class international management library which participants are encouraged to use.''

Our analysis of this course in terms of its relationship with learning styles is that, as described, it would relate in the following ways:-

Theorist: The course description is strongly related to the Theorist's needs for systems, concepts, inter-relationships of ideas and events and dealing with complexity.

The statement of objectives would, in itself, be persuasive to a Theorist, since it seems to be authoritative and well rounded.

Pragmatist: The general statements of objectives might not be fully persuasive to a Pragmatist; they would probably be insufficiently clearly related to his preferences for direct links to his job. He would be more influenced by an examination of detailed course content, for which we do not have room here.

Reflector: The Reflector would apparently have to define and make many of his own Reflector experiences on this course. There is no indication that the course is explicitly structured to meet at least half of his needs.

While he will enjoy the opportunity to analyse case studies, some of his other characteristics might make the course a difficult experience. The Reflector, carrying out his listening/observing on a course not designed to aid that process explicitly, is at risk of being seen as a low contributor. He could be a good ''source of feedback'' to others if he carried out his preferred style; but how effective will others be in giving feedback to him?

Activist: The emphasis on the general environment, on case discussions and analysis, and on ''a substantial volume of reading'' and the lack of emphasis on here and now acivities suggest that an Activist will not be happy with a lot of the course processes.

All these comments derive from the written material about the course; they would have to be tested against other evidence about the course, derived from visits or discussions with previous participants. Are the faculty really of the intellectual quality to attract the Theorist or are they alternatively at the level of plausibility to attract the Pragmatist? Is the course sufficiently geared to the immediate needs of the Pragmatist in terms of easily transferable techniques? How far does the course, in practice, provide protected opportunities for the

Reflector to review what he is learning – and if this is provided, what is done to prevent the Activist from running away?

A Marketing Course
Programme Content:

"The emphasis throughout the programme is on the integration of the various aspects of marketing into a coherent strategy, the co-ordination of marketing with other functions of the company, and the development of a symbiotic relationship between the company and its environment.

The opening segment of Strategic Marketing Management provides the opportunity for participants to develop an in-depth understanding of the key concepts which provide the foundations for successful marketing strategies. Here we emphasise topics such as demand analysis and demand management, the marketing mix, product portfolio analysis, and market segmentation. In addition, the tools of financial analysis are introduced so that they can be used throughout the programme.

During the middle segment of the programme, participants choose between two sections. One relates to the marketing of consumer goods and services and the other covers the marketing of industrial goods and services. This specialisation enables each participant to study issues and situations of maximum relevance to his or her responsibilities.

In both sections, specific situations studied will include companies active in a wide range of products and services.

The final portion of the programme examines the development and evolution of the marketing strategy including the assessment of major environmental changes, the analysis of competitive battles, and the management of strategy implementation.

Throughout the programme the emphasis is on rigorous analysis, careful strategy formulation, effective implementation, and meticulous monitoring and control."

Theorist: A course which emphasises strategy, co-ordination and the development of a symbiotic relationship will be attractive to Theorists. They will further be encouraged by the attention given to key concepts, and they will positively enjoy the opportunity to engage in "rigorous analysis".

Pragmatist: If the emphasis is too strongly on concepts and systems, particularly in the early stages of the programme, they may be less attracted than the Theorist. However, the emphasis on particular topics and the choice of specialisation should help them. This latter point is particularly important in supporting the choice of this course for a Pragmatist as compared with a course which did not offer this opportunity to study cases of more direct relevance. (A Theorist would be much less bothered by the absence of directly applicable material).

Reflector: The problem is again how far the course, which may suit them in giving them a chance to assimilate before commenting, offers them support for other aspects of their Reflector style. While the analysis of cases is congruent, is the 'hurly burly' of debate, even in small groups, likely to suit them? How will they respond to being asked to present their analysis to a large group of managers?

Activist: A strongly Activist oriented learner would be as much antagonised by the brochure as the Theorist might be encouraged. He might not get beyond the statement about "the symbiotic relationship between Company and its environment". However, the Activist probably would not read the brochure very carefully, if at all. If he went on the course, and the course was as described, he would be uncomfortable with rigorous analysis and meticulous monitoring and control. He would dislike the solitary work of reading cases, and would probably "take a ride" on others who had done the reading, participating volubly but superficially.

An Action Learning Programme

Action Learning has become a generic title for a number of activities not all of which would be recognised or accepted by Reg Revans as being genuine examples of his major contribution. We base the following interpretations on what Revans has said himself, and on what has been written about the G.E.C. versions of Action Learning. The interpretations do not necessarily apply to other versions of Action Learning, not all of which we suspect were designed with the same care and rigour.

Revans has said of Action Learning that it was designed: "to help each manager observe more keenly his present condition, by obliging him to list (for his colleagues) his goals, the obstructions that bar those goals, the means by which he intends to remove those obstructions".

Action Learning is based on his view that behavioural change is more likely to follow the reinterpretation of past experience than from the acquisition of fresh knowledge. It is also based on an understanding of learning as a social process; learners are helped to learn from each other.

Revans has no time for traditional management education or educators; in his approach the role of teachers is to contrive conditions in which managers may learn with and from each other. Crucially, Action Learning tackles real problems in real time in the real world; the problems are defined as a project, and the Learner collects the data necessary to help him and others resolve the problem.

Activist: The sense of participating in something relatively new would be attractive to Activists, as would the emphasis on tackling real problems. However, they would be irked by the length of the project, by the necessity to get clarification of terms of reference, by attempts to provide regularity and structure and by the process of reviewing what has been learned. An Activist might enjoy the project work; he would dislike the "set" discussions in which actions and learning are reviewed.

Reflector: A Reflector would appreciate some major features, especially the opportunity to produce carefully considered analyses, the process of reviewing what has occurred within the project and within the learning group, the reduction of risks during this latter process. He will enjoy the process of thinking things over, and the opportunity to give and receive feedback.

Theorist: A Theorist is likely to be attracted to some elements of Action Learning and repelled by others. He will like the opportunity of being stretched by a complex problem; he will probably appreciate, without always committing himself to, the theory behind Action Learning. He will probably however, increasingly find himself uneasy about concentration on a particular project, and the likely absence of a process of generalisation. Whatever the care with which the initial structure of the exercise is set up, it is likely to move into conditions of ambiguity, and uncertainty, conditions especially difficult for him.

Pragmatist: A Pragmatist would have difficulty, at least initially, with the original Revans version, involving people moving outside their own functions and their own organisations, since this would be insufficiently linked to perceived reality. If this is not an issue, two major aspects could be very attractive – the high face validity of tackling real problems, and the requirement to produce action plans. He would also participate happily in the process of exchanging ideas and problems with other learners as the project proceeds.

Some examples of how different the reactions of different individuals were to even the common parts of the learning experience, the project "set" discussions, can be seen from the Casey and Pearce book on Action Learning at G.E.C.

An Experience of Being Coached
Coaching is the process by which one person tries to guide another to improve his effectiveness. One example might be listening to a rehearsal of an important presentation and suggesting improvements; or going over a written report and highlighting ways in which it could better meet the interests of recipients. Coaching might be given by questioning, guidance or illustrative performance. It was proposed as a major and universal management need a few years ago. One of the reasons for the failure of this process to catch on widely was that it required managers to behave in ways which were unacceptable to them; another reason was that no attention was paid to the learning style of the recipient. Differences in learning style between the person giving, and the person receiving the coaching experience, are likely to be crucial. (Chapter 5 illustrates the general point).

Activist: He is unlikely to respond favourably to a direct tutorial coaching situation, in which skill or knowledge is explained or demonstrated; he would dislike the passive element. Nor would he be more responsive to non-direct coaching, the more subtle form in which a coach attempts to get points across through questions which cause the learner to review and learn from his own activities. He would be likely to see the approach as too analytical and long-winded – if indeed he recognised what was happening at all.

Reflector: The opportunity to watch someone else, or to review in a fairly well protected situation his own activities in response to questions would be welcomed. He would not respond so well to direct instruction – "do it this way", where he might want more evidence that that was the "right" way. He might be unhappy if asked to 'perform' without some preparation.

Theorist: He would probably respond well to a well prepared coaching situation whether direct tutorial or non-directive questioning, but would not respond to ad hoc sessions. He would require the basis of the coaching to be intellectually respectable, e.g. not simply being given a technique but being given an explanation of why it works, being given a chance to work out the value of the process in his own terms and not simply having to accept it from an authority figure (boss or teacher).

Pragmatist: He is likely to be highly responsive providing the subject matter has clear relevance to his own current performance, and providing the person offering the coaching is seen by him as authoritative. If the activity has high face validity the learner will participate in the process so eagerly that he may build on and improve what is being offered.

An Experience of Going Along with John
The process of learning called "sitting by Nellie" is still widely used. In the managerial environment it includes those occasions when a manager is given the opportunity to observe a more experienced colleague in action. We will take as an illustration a manager who attends a negotiation session with Trade Union representatives; he has no prime role but is attending because he will have the responsibility of negotiating at a later date. He is there to learn.

Before moving on to our analysis, the reader might like to pause and write down his own views on how each of Activist, Reflector, Theorist and Pragmatist might respond.

Activist: A strongly Activist learner would probably initially welcome the experience, especially if it was really novel to him and clearly related to his future role. He would be less attracted if he had experience previously of other negotiations situations. He would not be worried if the opportunity was given to him without warning. His actual learning response would be unlikely to be very effecive: he would be unhappy about being on the side lines and would not naturally think of ways in which he could make use of the experience. He would have to be given considerable guidance and help to overcome his natural style.

Reflector: This is a situation which the Reflector likes and can make use of. He will make best use of it if given prior notice so that he can think over what he will try to get out of the session, and organise his observation. He would not need to discuss his observation with anyone else. He would not require a lot of help beforehand, but would probably be happy to use help.

Theorist: The Theorist would benefit most if the session is carefully prepared, his own participation structured and if the existing company negotiator is, by the standards of the learner, highly competent. He is less likely to benefit if he is thrown in without warning; he will want to know what the history is, what the strategy is, what in precise terms he can learn from the session. If, however, the situation was new to him, his intellectual curiosity might make even an unprepared session potentially acceptable.

Pragmatist: Given the requirement to be involved in future negotiations the Pragmatist would welcome the opportunity, and would make effective use of either a planned or an unplanned opportunity. He would respond favourably to planning the experience beforehand and he would be unhappy if he was not given the chance to discuss the session afterwards.

Increasing the Range of Choice

In this chapter our main concern has been to help people make a more effective choice, given their currently predominant learning style. In many cases a major improvement in the use of time and energy can be secured by a better choice of learning activity, congruent with existing learning style. Some activities should be avoided by some people. However, in later chapters we show how learning styles may be expanded in some cases so that some individuals can take advantage of a wider range of opportunities.

Summary

We have shown in this chapter that, using our list of learning activities, it is possible to assess critically the content of various learning opportunities and see which learning styles are most likely to be well matched with them.

The actions we advocate are:-

● To look at those learning activities which dominate within a style.

● To assess the impact of these on identified learning needs.

● To determine which activities are most likely to be effective for a particular individual.

● To review which learning style is likely to be involved in various kinds of learning opportunity.

● To assess how this relates to the preferred style of an individual.

Chapter 4
How to use Learning Styles for Self Development

We believe the idea of self-development, which has come into vogue during the last ten years or so, is a very sound one. It stems from the realisation that each individual is ultimately responsible for, and in the best position to organise his own learning. Admittedly there are plenty of interested parties offering help (training departments, the Open University, technical colleges, self-help groups, etc.), but essentially they can only provide learning opportunities – it is up to the individual to decide whether to take advantage of the plethora of opportunities on offer. The old adage that you can lead a horse to water but you can't make it drink, accurately describes not only the behaviour of horses but also of human beings. We have therefore written this chapter for those who will tackle the L.S.Q. themselves, without the intervention or help of boss or specialist adviser. The L.S.Q., in common with other instruments of its type, will not force anyone to do anything but, used properly, it can help to start individuals off on the self-development trail and particularly will help identify which possibilities are likely to suit them best.

Let us assume that you, whoever you are and whatever you do, want to accept the challenge of developing yourself. This chapter aims to show you how to go about this with the L.S.Q. as your starting point. Unfortunately right at the outset you have a major decision to make. You have to decide between two quite different self-development aims. This is because the L.S.Q. offers you a choice. Either you can set out to become an all-round learner such that all four learning styles are within your repertoire, or you can decide to use the L.S.Q. as a basis for selecting learning opportunities that suit your existing style preferences. The decision is major because the self-development activities that stem from each choice are substantially different. For example, if you decide to work at becoming an all-round learner it inevitably involves identifying current gaps or weaknesses and doing something to improve them. If, on the other hand, you decide to leave your existing styles unaltered and to become more adept at choosing learning activities that are compatible (or avoiding activities that are incompatible) it involves building on strengths and living with your weaknesses.

Both options are entirely laudable. A decision to become an all-round learner is probably the tougher more demanding option and, if you were successful, equips you to take advantage of a wider range of different learning experiences. But, having said that, the alternative advantages of using your knowledge of your dominant style as the basis for choosing between different learning experiences are also considerable. Time would no longer be wasted attending inappropriate seminars or conferences and you might be able to juggle priorities in your work or in your extra-mural activities to reduce your exposure to unsuitable activities and increase time spent on suitable ones. This is clearly a far more efficient way of organising your time than using a hit and miss approach and wondering, vaguely, why you so often miss.

The remainder of this chapter will now split into two sections. First we look at how to use your L.S.Q. result to select self-development activities that are compatible with your style preferences. We start with this because, on balance, it is an easier option to tackle than aiming to become an all-round learner. In the second section starting on Page 43, we move on to examine the tougher option of using the L.S.Q. to help you achieve the aim of becoming an all-rounder. We would suggest that if your L.S.Q. result shows extremes of preference, either high or low, it might be best to start by becoming adept at selecting activities that suit your dominant styles. You could then progress more gradually to the challenges of exposing yourself to activities that will develop your low preference style(s). If, on the other hand, your L.S.Q. result reveals marginal preferences between styles you are likely to find it more feasible to embark on some fine tuning to become an all-round learner.

Section 1: Selecting Learning Opportunities That Suit Your Style
After you have completed an L.S.Q., scored it and applied the appropriate norms, you will know which are your preferred styles and the relative strengths of those preferences. Before proceeding you might like to consider the possibility of cross-checking your own result by inviting some colleagues (*anyone* who knows you well will do) to complete an L.S.Q. ticking and crossing the items to give a picture of the way they see you. If you do this it is unlikely that the resultant scores will match precisely with your own, simply because some of the L.S.Q. items probe underlying beliefs rather more than manifest ways of behaving. Obviously other people, however well they might know you, only have direct access to your characteristic ways of behaving and can only infer the presence or absence of certain beliefs. However, despite differences in actual scores, other people's perceptions of you should approximately match your own. The order in which the learning styles emerge should be similar. If, for example, your own L.S.Q. result puts the styles in the order 1st Reflector, 2nd Theorist, 3rd Pragmatist, 4th Activist, it would be alarming if someone else perceived you to be predominantly Activist with Theorist and Reflector trailing well behind. If there *is* a wide disparity then you had better do an item by item comparison to see which you ticked that others crossed and vice versa. This in itself will not of course resolve any differences of opinion, but at least it will highlight where major contradictions occur and give you an opportunity to reconsider your own L.S.Q. or persuade people to reconsider their view of your behaviour patterns! (In the next chapter we discuss how the views of your boss on your learning style may be acquired and used).

If we assume that you have established an L.S.Q. result which you see as valid,let us examine how to use it as a basis for deciding which learning opportunities are most likely to suit your style.

No single learning style has any overwhelming advantage over any other. They all have their own strengths and weaknesses. (Though it is important to be cautious about labelling strengths and weaknesses since, to some extent, which is which depends on the context in which they are viewed). In summary, we see the relative strengths and weaknesses of each style as follows:-

Activist
Strengths:
Flexible and open minded.
Happy to have a go.
Happy to be exposed to new situations.
Optimistic about anything new and therefore unlikely to resist change.

Weaknesses:
Tendency to take the immediately obvious action without thinking.
Often take unnecessary risks.
Tendency to do too much themselves and hog the limelight.
Rush into action without sufficient preparation.
Get bored with implementation/consolidation.

Reflector
Strengths:
Careful.
Thorough and methodical.
Thoughtful.
Good at listening to others and assimilating information.
Rarely jump to conclusions.

Weaknesses:
Tendency to hold back from direct participation.
Slow to make up their minds and reach a decision.
Tendency to be too cautious and not take enough risks.
Not assertive – they aren't particularly forthcoming and have no 'small talk'.

Theorist
Strengths:
Logical 'vertical' thinkers.
Rational and objective.
Good at asking probing questions.
Disciplined approach.

Weaknesses:
Restricted in lateral thinking.
Low tolerance for uncertainty, disorder and ambiguity.
Intolerant of anything subjective or intuitive.
Full of 'shoulds, oughts and musts'.

Pragmatist
Strengths:
Keen to test things out in practice.
Practical, down to earth, realistic.
Businesslike – gets straight to the point.
Technique oriented.

Weaknesses:
Tendency to reject anything without an obvious application.
Not very interested in theory or basic principles.
Tendency to seize on the first expedient solution to a problem.
Impatient with waffle.
On balance, task oriented not people oriented.

It helps to be clear about the relative strengths and weaknesses of each style because selecting appropriate learning opportunities essentially involves finding activities where strengths will be utilised and where weaknesses will not prove too much of a handicap. The activity lists given in the previous chapter (Pages 25 to 29) are an invaluable aid for checking the compatibility of a learning activity with the strengths and weaknesses of each style. In the light of your L.S.Q. result you might like to reduce these lists to a few key questions that you can use to assess the appropriateness or otherwise of any learning opportunity that comes your way. Four or five key questions would probably suffice and here are some that we suggest could reveal relevant information depending on your style preference.

42

Key questions for Activists
● Shall I learn something new, i.e. that I didn't know/couldn't do before?
● Will there be a wide variety of different activities? (I don't want to sit and listen for more than an hour at a stretch!).
● Will it be O.K. to have a go/let my hair down/make mistakes/have fun?
● Shall I encounter some tough problems and challenges?
● Will there be other like-minded people to mix with?

Key questions for Reflectors
● Shall I be given adequate time to consider, assimilate and prepare?
● Will there be opportunities/facilities to assemble relevant information?
● Will there be opportunities to listen to other people's points of view – preferably a wide cross section of people with a variety of views?
● Shall I be under pressure to be slapdash or to extemporize?

Key questions for Theorists
● Will there be lots of opportunities to question?
● Do the objectives and programme of events indicate a clear structure and purpose?
● Shall I encounter complex ideas and concepts that are likely to stretch me?
● Are the approaches to be used and concepts to be explored 'respectable', i.e. sound and valid?
● Shall I be with people of similar calibre to myself?

Key questions for Pragmatists
● Will there be ample opportunities to practice and experiment?
● Will there be lots of practical tips and techniques?
● Shall we be addressing *real* problems and will it result in action plans to tackle some of *my* current problems?
● Shall we be exposed to experts who know how to/can do it themselves?

These questions, supplemented with any others that occur to you as you study the activity lists on Pages 25 to 29, should help you pick and choose more successfully between different learning opportunities.

If your L.S.Q. result indicates that you have two or more learning style preferences then you will need to *combine* some of the key questions. For example, if you are a Reflector/Theorist you need to ask: "Shall I be given adequate time to consider, assimilate and prepare *and* will there be lots of opportunities to question?" If you are an Activist/Pragmatist you will need to ask: "Shall I learn something new *and* will there be ample opportunities to practice and experiment?" Another combination that frequently occurs is Theorist/Pragmatist in which case you need to ask: "Do the objectives and programme of events indicate a clear structure *and* shall we be addressing real problems?" If your L.S.Q. result shows you are already an all-rounder learner then you'll need to ask *all* the questions!

To summarise, the steps we advocate in order to use the L.S.Q. to select learning activities that are likely to prove compatible with your style are as follows:-

1. Do an L.S.Q., score it and apply the appropriate norms.

2. Cross check your result by getting someone else (who knows you well) to do an L.S.Q. on your behalf.

3. Discuss big and/or surprising discrepancies.

4. In the light of your L.S.Q. result, list your relative strengths and weaknesses using the lists on Pages 40 and 41.

5. Study the activity lists on Pages 25 to 29 to see which activities are compatible and incompatible with your style(s).

6. Thereafter, whenever possible, before indulging in a learning activity, get answers to the appropriate key questions on Page 42.

7. Go ahead with the activity if you are satisfied it dovetails sufficiently with your style.

Section 2: Becoming an All-Round Learner

For the remainder of this chapter let us turn our attention to the mechanics of modifying your learning styles such that you bring Activist, Reflector, Theorist and Pragmatist into a neck and neck relationship with one another. As we acknowledged earlier in this chapter, this is probably a tougher challenge than merely selecting learning activities that are consonant with your prevailing styles. The advantage of succeeding is that a broad repertoire of styles better equips you to benefit from a wide range of different learning activities. It is the equivalent of firing on all four learning cylinders rather than moving along on one or two.

It is best to start with a careful analysis of the L.S.Q. items you have crossed. This is because crossed items indicate things you do not do or believe in and are, therefore, a pointer to what you will need to practise in order to become an all-rounder. Of course some of the crosses may have been marginal, i.e. the balance between being more in disagreement than in agreement with an item was finely poised but, since you had to go one way or the other, you crossed rather than ticked it. Other crosses will indicate more strongly held responses. It is, therefore, a good idea to list the crossed items within a style in two groups; strong and less strong. It also helps to express crossed items negatively: so if, for example, item 2 'I often throw caution to the winds' was crossed then it is best to list it as 'I *do not* often throw caution to the winds'. Here is an example of this listing process assuming a low Activist score of 6.

Crossed Activist Items
A. Strong (i.e. consistently like me in a whole variety of situations).

2. I *do not* often 'throw caution to the winds'.

10. I *do not* actively seek out new experiences.

23. I *do not* thrive on the challenge of tackling something new and different.

32. I *do not* tend to be open about how I'm feeling.

43. In discussions I *do not* usually pitch in with lots of 'off-the-top-of-the-head' ideas.

48. On balance I *do not* talk more than I listen.

58. I *do not* enjoy being the one that talks a lot.

72. I'm *not* usually the 'life and soul' of the party.

B. Less strong (i.e. still typical of me but only in specific situations).

4. I *do not* believe that formal procedures and policies cramp people's style.

17. I'm *not* attracted more to novel, unusual ideas than to practical ones.

24. I *do not* enjoy fun-loving spontaneous people.

34. I *do not* prefer to respond to events on a spontaneous basis rather than plan things out in advance.

71. I *do not* find the formality of having specific objectives and plans stifling.

79. I *do not* enjoy the drama and excitement of a crisis situation.

A list as long as this with, in this case, fourteen crossed items might seem rather daunting but you might be able to narrow it down by identifying some priorities for self-development. You could do this by grouping items in a similar vein together so, for example, items 2, 10, 23 group together and are indicative of being cautious about anything new or different. Similarly, items 32, 43, 48, 58, 72 group together suggesting a tendency to be inhibited and reticent. Items 4, 34, 71 form a third group, the link here being a tendency to cling to pre-arranged plans and procedures rather than being spontaneous and opportunistic. Searching for themes amongst crossed items helps to narrow down the options and focus your self-development activities.

Another way to identify self-development priorities is to view crossed L.S.Q. items in the light of the demands of your current or future occupation. If, for example, you frequently have to attend meetings where problems are 'brainstormed' you might put a high priority on item 43 (At meetings I usually pitch in with lots of off-the-top-of-the-head ideas). If, to give another example, you are in a 'fire-fighting', 'trouble-shooting' sort of job where you have to respond to a whole host of urgent problems, you would presumably put item 79 (I enjoy the drama and excitement of a crisis situation) high on your list.

For self-development purposes it is best to list crossed L.S.Q. items for any learning style where the L.S.Q. gives you a score which, according to the norms you apply, is below average. Using the general norms (on Page 75) to illustrate this, you would list crossed items for an Activist score of 8 and below, for a Reflector score of 13 and below and for a Theorist and Pragmatist score of 12 and below. Even if your L.S.Q. result puts all your scores above the average this does not, of course, preclude you from earmarking some crossed items that you would like to develop or strengthen. Deciding which items to develop in order to become an all-round learner has to be your decision and once made it gives your self-development project a sense of direction, or, if you like, an objective.

Having identified some self-development objectives the next step is to plan some self-development activities. The plans must be feasible rather than 'pie in the sky' and specific rather than 'airy fairy'. In effect, self-development plans are a commitment to encourage yourself to do something which you do not normally do. Feasibility and specificity help to ensure that the plan will be successful in prodding you into action. Clearly you are more likely to action the plan if you avoid flinging yourself in at the deep end. If you are a beginner it is best to start in the shallow end and graduate to deeper water. Depending on your starting point, some of the suggestions that follow might strike you as too ambitious. If so, you might like to break them down into smaller, more feasible steps. Since your development plans need to be tailor-made to suit your circumstances, we can only offer a variety of suggestions in the hope that they act as useful thought-starters. Here then are a few ideas for the strengthening of any, or all, of the four learning styles.

Thought-Starters:
Self-Development Activities to Strengthen the Activist Style.

● Do something new, i.e. something that you have never done before, at least once each week. Hitch a lift to work, visit a part of your organisation you have neglected, go jogging at lunch time, wear something outrageous to work one day, read an unfamiliar newspaper with views that are diametrically opposed to yours, change the layout of furniture in your office, etc.

● Practice initiating conversations (especially 'small talk') with strangers. Select people at random from your internal telephone directory and go and talk to them. At large gatherings, conferences or parties, force yourself to initiate and sustain conversations with *everyone* present. In your spare time go door to door canvassing for a cause of your choice.

● Deliberately fragment your day by chopping and changing activities each half hour. Make the switch as diverse as possible. For example, if you have had half an hour of cerebral activity, switch to doing something utterly routine and mechanical. If you have been sitting down, stand up. If you have been talking, keep quiet, and so on.

● Force yourself into the limelight. Volunteer whenever possible to chair meetings or give presentations. When you attend a meeting set yourself the challenge of making a substantial contribution within 10 minutes of the start of the meeting. Get on a soapbox and make a speech at Speakers' Corner.

● Practice thinking aloud and on your feet. Set yourself a problem and bounce ideas off a colleague (see if between you you can generate 50 ideas in 10 minutes). Get some colleagues/friends to join in a game where you give each other topics and have to give an impromptu speech lasting at least 5 minutes.

Thought-Starters:
Self-Development Activities to Strengthen the Reflector Style.

● Practice observing, especially at meetings where there are agenda items that do not directly involve you. Study people's behaviour. Keep records about who does the most talking, who interrupts whom, what triggers disagreements, how often the chairman summarises and so on. Also study non-verbal behaviour. When do people lean forward and lean back? Count how many times people emphasise a point with a gesture. When do people fold their arms, look at their watches, chew their pencils and so on?

● Keep a diary and each evening write an account of what happened during the day. Reflect on the day's events and see if you can reach any conclusions from them. Record your conclusions in the diary.

● Practice reviewing after a meeting or event of some kind. Go back over the sequence of events identifying what went well and what could have gone better. If possible tape record some conversations and play back the tape at least twice, reviewing what happened in great detail. List lessons learned from this activity.

● Give yourself something to research, something that requires the pains-taking gathering of data from different sources. Go to your local library and spend a few hours in the reference section.

● Practice producing highly polished pieces of writing. Give yourself essays to write on various topics (something you have researched?). Write a report or paper about something. Draft watertight policy statements, agreements or procedures. When you have written something, put it aside for a week then force yourself to return to it and do a substantial rewrite.

● Practice drawing up lists for and against a particular course of action. Take a contentious issue and produce balanced arguments from both points of view. Whenever you are with people who want to rush into action, caution them to consider alternatives and to anticipate the consequences.

Thought-Starters:
Self-Development Activities to Strengthen the Theorist Style.

● Read something 'heavy' and thought provoking for at least 30 minutes each day. Try philosophy, especially linguistic analysis, logic or the theory of relativity. If this seems a tall order, try tackling a text book on management or read Thouless on 'Straight and Crooked Thinking'. Whatever you elect to read, afterwards try to summarise what you have read in your own words.

● Practice spotting inconsistencies/weaknesses in other people's arguments. Go through reports highlighting inconsistencies. Analyse organisation charts to discover overlaps and conflicts. Take two newspapers of different persuasions and regularly do a comparative analysis of the differences in their points of view.

● Take a complex situation and analyse it to pinpoint why it developed the way it did, what could have been done differently and at what stage. The situations could be historical or something drawn from current affairs, or something you have been involved in personally. You could, for example, do a detailed analysis of how you spend your time, or of the work flow in and out of your department, or of all the people you interact with and with what frequency in the course of your work.

● Collect other people's theories, hypotheses and explanations about events; they might be about environmental issues, theology, the natural sciences, human behaviour – *anything* providing it is a topic with many different, and preferably contradictory, theories. Try to understand the underlying assumptions each theory is based upon and see if you can group similar theories together.

● Practice structuring situations so that they are orderly and more certain to proceed in the way you predict. You might, for example, plan a conference where delegates are going to work in different groupings. Structure the timetable, the tasks, the plenary sessions. Or try structuring a meeting by having a clear purpose, an agenda and a planned beginning, middle and end. Invent procedures to cope with problems such as too many people speaking at once or failures to reach a consensus.

● Practice asking probing questions – the sort of questions that get to the bottom of things. Refuse to be fobbed off with platitudes or vague answers. Particularly ask questions designed to find out precisely why something has occurred: "Why do you think the machine has gone down again?" "Why is absenteeism increasing?" "Why do more women than men smoke?" "Why is heart disease higher in the U.K. than in Japan?"

Thought-Starters:
Self-Development Activities to Strengthen the Pragmatist Style.

● Collect techniques, i.e. practical ways of doing things. The techniques can be about anything potentially useful to you. They might be analytical techniques such as critical path analysis or cost benefit analysis. They might be interpersonal techniques such as Transactional Analysis, or Assertiveness or presentation techniques. They might be time saving techniques or statistical techniques, or techniques to improve your memory, or techniques to cope with stress and reduce your blood pressure!

● In meetings and discussions of any kind (progress meetings, problem solving meetings, planning meetings, appraisal discussions, negotiations, sales calls etc.), concentrate on producing action plans. Make it a rule never to emerge from a meeting or discussion without a list of actions either for yourself or for others or both. The action plans should be specific and include a deadline (e.g. "I will produce chapter 4 by 31st May". "Bill will produce a 2 page paper listing alternative bonus schemes by 1st September".).

- Make opportunities to experiment with some of your new found techniques. Try them out in practice. If your experiment involves other people then tell them openly that you are conducting an experiment and explain the technique which is about to be tested. (This reduces embarrass-ment if, in the event, the technique is a flop!). Choose the time and place for your experiments. Avoid situations where a lot is at stake and where the risks of failure are unacceptably high. Experiment in routine settings with people whose aid or support you can enlist.

- Study techniques that other people use and then model yourself on them. Pick up techniques from your boss, your boss's boss, your colleagues, your subordinates, visiting salesmen, interviewers on television, politicians, actors and actresses, your next door neighbour. When you discover something they do well – emulate them.

- Subject yourself to scrutiny from 'experts' so that they can watch your technique and coach you in how to improve it. Invite someone who is skilled in running meetings to sit in and watch you chairing, get an accomplished presenter to give you feedback on your presentation techniques. The idea is to solicit help from people who have a proven track record – it's the equivalent of having a coaching session with a golfing professional.

- Tackle a 'do-it-yourself' project – it doesn't matter if you aren't good with your hands. Pragmatists are practical and, if only for practice purposes, D.I.Y. activities help to develop a practical outlook. Renovate a piece of furniture, build a garden shed or even an extension to your house. At work, calculate your own statistics once in a while instead of relying on the printout, be your own organisation and methods man, go and visit the shop floor in search of practical problems to solve. Learn to type, learn a foreign language.

To conclude this section we reaffirm that whatever your existing learning style preferences, they are subject to adjustment. This can either happen by accident as, for example, would occur if you changed your job or acquired a new boss with a markedly different style from his predecessor, or it can happen deliberately as part of a self-development plan. We hope the suggestions in this section open your eyes to this latter possibility and stimulate you into taking action. The learning skills you have already acquired are unlikely to be harmed or to diminish as a result of this process. Indeed the whole idea is to *add* to your repertoire and become a fully equipped all-round learner.

This chapter should have given you plenty of ideas about how to use knowledge of your learning styles for self-development purposes. Whether you decide to turn yourself into an all-round learner or to be more rigorous in selecting learning activities that suit your existing style(s), we hope to have demonstrated how the L.S.Q. provides you with a useful starting point.

The ideas given here for individuals are extended in the work book, 'Using Your Learning Styles', which gives more details of activities you can undertake.

Chapter 5

How the Boss Can Use Learning Styles

Introduction
So far we have been concerned to explain how an understanding of his own dominant learning styles can help an individual help himself to learn more effectively. In this chapter we concentrate on the individual's boss; although many of the things we say apply also to the way in which colleagues too could help, we have not specifically covered their role.

The boss has a prime role in identifying and making use of learning opportunities. We have not repeated here a full discussion of how a boss or colleague can help others to learn (see Mumford "Making Experience Pay"). In this chapter we want to show how a knowledge of the learning styles of his subordinates can help a boss choose from these opportunities more effectively.

First we show how the boss can make use of his knowledge of learning styles in helping a subordinate choose whether to expand his style. Secondly, we show how an awareness by the boss of his own style can make him more conscious of what he is, and what he is not, likely to offer his subordinates in terms of learning experiences.

We presume that many of the readers of this manual will be in the position of having to show a boss why he should be interested in using knowledge of the learning styles of his subordinates. The answer is that he can provide more effective learning, more economically, if he knows which activities are likely to help particular individuals. Would a boss send someone on a Business School Programme, at a cost of say £7,000, if he knew the person was an Activist with a style highly different from that permeating the course? Would he recommend an experience of sitting in on a negotiation to someone with a low Reflector score?

Knowledge of Learning Styles of Others
We have shown in earlier chapters how different learning styles help to determine the effectiveness of particular learning activities for particular individuals. The previous chapter has shown how an individual can use that information for himself. That information may also be given to the individual's boss in order to help him understand his subordinate's likely approach to the different kinds of learning activity, and therefore to assist the boss to help him to choose activities in the light of his preferences. Most particularly, we want to help bosses avoid the Shakespeare effect in which an early inappropriate experience puts people off for life.

If the L.S.Q. results are uniformly high for an individual, he is likely to be able to learn from any kind of learning experience. If, however, the L.S.Q. shows both high and low scores then, as shown in the previous chapter, there is a question of whether the individual should be helped to improve the range of his effective learning behaviour or whether, instead, he should be helped to choose only those activities congruent with his existing dominant style.

We are convinced that learning behaviour, like other forms of managerial behaviour, can often be changed in a desired direction. However, the thought and effort required for this will be more than many managers are willing to invest, particularly at the time of their first experience with the use of learning styles. Willingness to invest is related to the learning style of the boss. For example, an Activist may be either insufficiently persuaded by the relevance of learning styles, or too impatient to work constructively at discussing alternatives with subordinates. If a Pragmatist finds that there is some return for him from the improved learning capacity of his subordinate, then he may be prepared to make the effort. It is also more likely that a boss will suggest the broadening of style approach if that involves movement towards his own dominant style.

Should the Subordinate Expand His Style?
The boss can help his subordinate firstly by assisting in the choice between these two basic approaches. The basis for the choice should always be what the subordinate wants, not what the boss feels to be right. This statement will be self-evident to most management development specialists, but not to many managers who are often decisive and authoritarian, rather than consultative, in style. The boss can sometimes usefully suggest by encouragement and the offer of help, that the subordinate tries to expand his range rather than simply accepting it. While it may seem self-evident to the boss that an Activist would benefit by being encouraged to read some books on management theory, or that a Reflector should make himself more dominant and visible, prescriptive solutions of this kind are unlikely to work.

A much more appropriate action would be first to discuss with the subordinate the validity of the L.S.Q. results; do they reflect the reality of the subordinate as they perceive it to be? Our experience is that sometimes one or the other will be slightly surprised at the results, but that this is usually based on the appearance of the words Activist or Theorist and that disagreement disappears when the descriptions are studied more carefully. Once agreement on validity is reached, then it is possible to start the discussion on whether to try and increase the range of learning styles, or to accept the dominant style.

Given the short time likely to be available for a discussion on whether or not to broaden, and also given the fact that most bosses are unlikely to be skilled in helping their subordinates to increase their range, it is most likely that the best and most acceptable line would be for the boss to suggest that the individual looks at the developmental actions set out in the previous chapter. If they look at these suggestions together, it may be that the individual would want to try one of them. The most productive situation would be that the subordinate should suggest action himself, and that the boss, if he agrees, should give encouragement or help.

We have too little evidence, so far, to be certain whether it would, in general, be productive for a boss to lean towards the approach of suggesting that the subordinate tries to increase his range. It is likely, in our view, that this would be more productive for Pragmatists and Reflectors than for Activists, because the latter may be unconvinced about the whole learning style approach. Reasons why the individual himself may choose one rather than the other approach are given in the previous chapter.

Whether he is helping the subordinate to broaden his range, or is helping him to choose activities within his range, the boss is providing initial psychological reward by agreeing with a proposed activity and then continuing the reward by subsequent reinforcement, i.e. by showing continued commitment and interest. Although a major reward for the learner will be in his own improved performance, the role of the boss is crucial in providing proof of whether the improved performance is worthwhile.

The boss can also provide help in the form of identifying and using different learning opportunities. Where the opportunities are within his own domain he may only have to make the necessary decision, for example that his subordinate should accompany him on a visit to an important customer, in order to increase his opportunities to observe others in action. In other cases however, he might have to persuade others or secure help; an appointment as secretary to a committee, or a recommendation for a particular course, or identification of the best recent book on Marketing, might involve the boss in going to other people.

In summary, the boss should:-

● Review the L.S.Q. results for his subordinate.

● Consider whether expansion or congruence should be the objective.

● Check the relevance of his own style to what he can do with his subordinate.

● Check what kind of learning opportunities he can provide or sponsor.

The Choice of Activities Congruent with Styles

While our values, our experiences and our recognition of the potential for improved performance incline us to suggest that managers should, in most cases, try to help subordinates increase their range, we recognise that many managers will not want to do this. They are more likely to be attracted by the relatively more simple process of identifying activities which are congruent with the dominant style and choosing those instead of choosing activities which are not congruent.

The boss may be either trying to think of relevant development opportunities as a result of an appraisal or a development discussion, or he may be responding to a suggestion that a particular kind of opportunity might be suitable. Many of the potential activities are set out in previous chapters, and the full list is not repeated here. A few illustrations are given to reinforce the point.

Case A

A manager has received details of two seminars on formal organisational processes for employee involvement in major managerial decisions. One seminar emphasises the quality of speakers, including well-known names from the European Commission; the other seminar emphasises the provision of a number of practical exercises designed to show the issues which will arise. He has a subordinate general manager who is currently under pressure to introduce a form of structured employee involvement; they are both agreed that some form of training would be relevant. L.S.Q. results show a high Pragmatist and low Theorist. They review the alternatives together and agree that the latter seminar fits the learning style the best (other issues about the choice are omitted here).

Case B

A manager has a senior assistant who attends a number of important meetings on budgets and plans with him. It is the manager's style to ask his subordinates for comments about the meeting. The subordinate is careful, analytical and relatively low profile at meetings, not giving to taking risks. He and his boss agree, during a development discussion, that he may perhaps have too low a visibility from the point of view of other people's perception of his current contribution and potential for other jobs. He has a high Reflector and a low Activist score. They agree together to make use of his high R. Instead of simply encouraging him to take a more active role, he will seek, and his boss will offer, feedback on the nature and effectiveness of the contributions he actually makes.

The significance of this case is that the chosen method is acceptable to both boss and subordinate; if either boss or subordinate had been high Activist, it is less likely that this process would have been either agreed or implemented.

We have chosen only two cases to illustrate the role of the boss since otherwise we would repeat the essence of the points made earlier in Chapter 3 showing the relationship between learning styles and learning effectiveness.

The Influence of the Learning Style of the Boss

So far we have shown how the boss can make use of his knowledge of the learning style of his subordinate, and we have referred only briefly to the influence of his own style, particularly when we talked about the general issue of how the style of the boss may affect what he does about the general question of whether a subordinate should attempt to broaden his style.

We turn now to a wider review of the way in which the learning style of the boss will influence what he does in helping others to learn. Our general proposition is that a boss, if he encourages learning at all, will tend to do so in ways consonant with his own learning style. This is more clearly true for those activities in which he has a direct involvement himself. That is to say that, for example, an Activist boss will provide experience of immediate response to situations, will gaily throw subordinates in at the deep end. He will not personally provide highly systematic and analytical experiences. In the next few pages we set out what a boss is likely to provide or encourage personally. We want, however, to emphasise at this point that a boss may well be responsive to suggestions from others about the provision of opportunities which are not congruent with his own style. While, for example, an Activist boss will be impatient with structured and systematic approaches to learning for others as well as for himself, a strongly Theorist boss could be persuaded that a learning activity appropriate to a Reflector would be useful for a subordinate even though he would not learn from it himself.

We have gone into detail about what the boss is likely to provide himself because of the pre-eminent role of the boss in learning on the job. What he provides or accepts outside his own direct involvement with his subordinate is most important and, in many cases, crucial (because of what he does not provide himself), but it is essentially second in importance.

The Activist Boss
Activists will tend to help by:-

- Generating (unconsciously) opportunities for others to observe and reflect on what they do.

- Taking an optimistic and positive view of what is involved in a new situation.
- Giving a positive and encouraging lead, at least initially, in short term active learning activities.
- Taking a chance on exposing a subordinate to a new situation.
- Following through with action to provide learning experiences *if* they have been convinced of their value.
- Responding spontaneously to opportunities as they arise.

Activists will be less likely to provide help through:-

- Providing planned learning experiences.
- Giving support to learning as a planned, structured, activity.
- Assessing and using learning experiences which are different from those through which they learned.
- Discussing learning opportunities beforehand and reviewing them afterwards.
- Standing back and allowing others to participate or take action.
- Giving a good personal model of planned learning behaviour.
- Giving different learning experiences to subordinates with different learning styles.

The Reflector Boss
Reflectors will tend to help by:-

- Suggesting activities which can be observed.
- Recommending how observation can be carried out.
- Identifying ways in which an event or a problem can be analysed.
- Discussing what may happen, and reviewing what has happened.
- Providing data or feedback in a controlled learning situation.
- Advising on how to prepare carefully for a management activity.
- Not taking a dominant role in meetings with subordinates.
- Emphasising the importance of collecting data before acting.
- Giving a considered response to requests for help.

Reflectors will be less likely to provide help through:-

● Suggesting ad hoc immediate learning opportunities.

● Showing how to take advantage spontaneously of unplanned learning activities.

● Providing unexpected or slightly risky learning situations, e.g. a sudden delegation of a task.

● Giving immediate answers to unexpected requests for direct help.

● Providing a large scale view of philosophy, concept, system or policy.

● Providing a strong personal model of anything except Reflector behaviour.

The Theorist Boss
Theorists will tend to help by:-

● Showing interest in any intellectually respectable idea.

● Helping people to describe underlying causes, to explain the systems or concepts involved in an activity.

● Demonstrating the intellectual validity of an answer or process.

● Showing how to strengthen or demolish a case by the use of logic.

● Bringing out complexities.

● Aiming for clarity of structure of purpose.

● Articulating theories, e.g. Open Systems Theory or Theory X and Theory Y.

● Generalising reasons why something works or does not work.

● Setting high standards in the quality of data.

Theorists will be less likely to provide help through:-

● Showing when to accept the obvious.

● Helping others to understand emotions and feelings in specific circumstances.

● Making use of data or occasions which conflict with their theories.

● Developing others who are different in intellectual quality or style, e.g. if perceived as lower calibre, or if theories clash with their own.

● Showing how to use information which *they* regard as trivial, irrelevant or intellectually not respectable.

● Drawing up specific action plans.

The Pragmatist Boss
Pragmatists will tend to help by:-

● Showing responsiveness to new ideas and techniques.

● Demonstrating interest in specific action plans.

● Pressing for relevant learning programmes with clear pay off.

● Being open to new situations.

● Showing a belief in the possibility of improvement.

● Following the party line on, e.g. appraisals or releasing people for courses.

● Following specific suggestions on how to improve learning.

Pragmatists will be less likely to provide help through:-

● Being responsive to ideas or techniques not immediately relevant to a current problem.

● Showing interest in concepts or theories.

● Encouraging action relevant to the longer term.

● Encouraging ideas or learning programmes that they regard as unproven or way out.

● Pushing for action which is apparently not valued by the culture or system.

● Using learning opportunities which they see as divorced from real life, e.g. secondments outside the organisation, sessions by "people who don't know our kind of industry/organisation/problems".

Clearly, if the boss knows what kind of learning activities he is not likely to provide himself, he may be (and of course in terms of managerial responsibility, ought to be) at least responsive to suggestions outside his own style. The best bosses will indeed positively seek to fill in the gaps by using other people and resources.

In this chapter we will make a variety of suggestions about how the adviser can use L.S.Q. results to improve the effectiveness of training and development activities. We have used the term adviser to cover people in management education, training or development – indeed anyone whose professional role includes helping others to learn. The suggestions in this chapter vary in complexity. Some of them are simple to implement and integrate into existing training activities without undue upheaval. Other suggestions are more adventurous and, if adopted, are likely to involve major changes to both the structure and methodology of training programmes. Some of the suggestions included in this chapter have been tried and tested by us over the last couple of years. Other suggestions are planned but not yet implemented and still others are but a twinkle in our eyes.

We will divide our ideas for using learning styles in this chapter into five different sections. We start with suggestions about how the adviser can build the L.S.Q. into development discussions. We then look at how trainers can use the L.S.Q. before, during and after training programmes. Finally we look at how the L.S.Q. can help the adviser to analyse his or her own style preferences and the implications this has for facilitating the learning of others.

Although the most obvious application of the L.S.Q. may seem to be on courses, many of the examples used in this manual show how it can be used in a variety of on the job situations. Most of this chapter is aimed at helping the person running courses. We do not need to repeat all the illustrations given earlier of ways in which the L.S.Q. can be used outside the course context in a wider management development role. We have already covered:-

- The use of the L.S.Q. in improving the dialogue between the learner and others about his likely response to different kinds of learning activity, using the check lists shown on Pages 25 to 29.

- The use of the L.S.Q. in clarifying both the need and the possibility of broadening an individual's range of learning styles.

- The process by which the learning content of particular activities can be assessed, and how this can be used to help individuals.

- The use of L.S.Q. results in identifying the kind of learning opportunities likely to be provided by particular managers, and therefore their suitability in promoting learning in other individuals, using the lists shown on Pages 55 to 58.

Using the L.S.Q. in a Development Discussion

The L.S.Q. is particularly valuable when used as part of a discussion on individual development needs rather than as an isolated diagnostic instrument. One of the authors has frequently used it by getting 'clients' to complete a questionnaire as preparation for a development discussion. The process of scoring and interpreting the L.S.Q. result opens up useful discussion and widens people's understanding of the variety of learning opportunities available. Discussion then centres on selecting development activities to suit or broaden their styles. The kind of results which can be secured are illustrated by two cases:-

Manager A was a newly appointed General Manager. In the course of a discussion about his performance he said that he felt there were some gaps in his functional experience, and in his ability to develop a strategic view which he would like to remedy. He had heard that a management programme might help him, but he said he was cynical about courses because his past experiences with them had been poor. His L.S.Q. results were Activist 8, Reflector 14, Theorist 16, Pragmatist 18. He was, in fact, sent on a major Business School course, and reported very favourably on it; his post course report brought out the issues of relevance of content and quality of the lecturers, which would be predicted by his L.S.Q.

Manager B had been promoted when relatively young and inexperienced. While in principle he accepted he still had a lot to learn, he also needed to show that he had a directly useful contribution to make. He had a low Reflector score, a result he was initially inclined to challenge. Further discussion on this revealed ways in which he could, without making a fundamental change in his normal behaviour, increase his Reflector activities after some of the meetings in which he was involved.

Using Learning Styles Before a Training Programme

1. *To help with the identification of training needs.*

    The L.S.Q. can be used as part of a survey to identify training needs. We believe that information about the characteristic learning styles of any target population – be they apprentices, clerical trainees, graduates or managers – is always worth collecting and taking into acount before designing a piece of training. One of the authors was recently involved in a training needs analysis exercise where all the managers throughout the whole organisation were surveyed. The L.S.Q. was included in the survey along with other questionnaires aimed at surfacing management training requirements. Prior to the L.S.Q. results being known, the Company Training Manager had assumed that a fairly standard management skills course would fit the bill. Indeed he had even held preliminary discussions with a number of external training organisations and briefed them on the likely contents of the course he envisaged. However, once the L.S.Q. results were known the Training Manager was persuaded to have second thoughts. In summary, the L.S.Q. results showed that the predominant learning style amongst managers in the company was Pragmatist. There were, however, important differences hierachically. For example, the company directors and senior managers were by far the most Pragmatic, with Activist a strong back-up style. Middle and first level managers on the other hand had Theorist as their back-up style with Reflector next and Activist last.

These results indicated quite clearly that a tailor-made management development activity for this particular company needed to have the following ingredients to be accepted by, and useful for, the majority of managers.

● It must, *above all,* be practical to appeal to the strong Pragmatic preferences.

● It must be soundly based and robust enough to survive the perfectionist scrutiny of the Theorists at middle and junior levels.

● It must be sufficiently novel and exciting to retain the enthusiastic involvement of the Activists at senior levels.

The idea of setting up a conventional series of off-the-job management training courses was now rejected on the grounds that it would not appeal strongly enough to the Pragmatists nor would it be novel enough to win commitment from the Activists at the top. Instead, a formula that combined training and development with problem solving project work was arrived at by setting up a whole series of project groups to work on real issues under the guidance of a number of external trainers. This was seen to meet the needs identified by the L.S.Q. by being:-

● Practical enough for Pragmatists.

● Soundly based for Theorists.

● Novel for Activists.

● Paced to suit the needs of the Reflectors (with four week gaps between sessions).

2. *To screen course members before they attend a training course.*
The L.S.Q. can easily be incorporated into the nomination procedures before people attend in-company training programmes of various kinds.

The L.S.Q. is sent out with an accompanying letter to prospective course members and returned to the training department for scoring and interpretation. Once the learning styles have been established a number of possibilities offer themselves. At the very least, advance warning about the predominant styles of the people coming together on a given course is useful for the trainer. It helps him/her prepare for the course and possibly slant parts of the programme to accommodate better the learning style preferences of the group. If there are a number of interchangeable trainers available to run a given programme then the trainer's style can be taken into account to get the most compatible match between trainees and trainer.

A rather more ambitious possibility is to use the L.S.Q. information to allocate certain people to certain courses. For example,if it was felt desirable to have together on one course an equal number of Activists, Reflectors, Theorists and Pragmatists, this can be engineered by administering some sort of quota system. This ensures that the group, as a whole, is well balanced with all the different learning skills equally represented. If, on the other hand, it is considered more practical to have as homogeneous a group as possible, then it is possible to invite, say, Activists/Pragmatists to attend one course together and Reflectors/ Theorists to attend on a different occasion. The courses, whilst attempting to achieve the same objectives, are easier to plan and run with the likes and dislikes/strengths and weaknesses of more homogeneous target populations clearly in mind. The syllabus therefore remains the same but the methods differ to cater for learning style preferences. Thus, there could, for example, be lots of projects for Activists, reading time built in for Reflectors, question and answer sessions for Theorists and practical demonstrations for Pragmatists.

If it is considered impractical to offer different versions of the same course, then it might be considered more feasible to design different options or branches within the same programme. The course contains some core activities standard for all irrespective, as it were, of differences in learning style preferences. At intervals, however, the programme splits into branching activities tailor-made to meet the needs of people with specific learning styles.

Using Learning Styles During a Training Programme
This section contains five different suggestions on how learning styles can be used to advantage during a training programme. The ideas are introduced in order of complexity starting with the simplest and progressing to the more substantial. The simple ideas are easy to 'graft on' to an existing training

course; the more complex ideas usually involve more fundamental design work.

1. *Predicting learning difficulties*
    If the L.S.Q. is administered and scored at the start of a training programme, at the most a half hour process, the trainer is in a better position to anticipate how course members are likely to behave during the course. For example, the L.S.Q. results help to anticipate who will:-

● Talk most and talk least.

● Ask questions and whether the questions will probe basic assumptions or explore applications.

● Find the course too fast/too slow.

● Volunteer to 'take the chair' or present in plenary sessions.

● Laugh most or be serious/earnest.

● Read handouts in the evenings or skimp them and prop up the bar instead.

● Produce lots of off-the-top-of-the-head ideas or only produce pre-prepared ones.

● Experiment with different ways of behaving or stick cautiously to the tried and true.

● Be keen to observe or be keen to take part.

● Welcome feedback or resist feedback.

Predictions like these are useful because they open up the possibility of a trainer being able to handle people more appropriately from the word go, rather than feeling his way for a period as people's behavioural tendencies gradually reveal themselves. So, for example, the L.S.Q. can help the trainer 'identify' which people need explicitly bringing-in to the proceedings and how best to answer questions to the satisfaction of the questioner. All this helps the trainer establish credibility with course members faster than might otherwise have been possible as well as helping them learn more effectively.

One of the authors has used the L.S.Q. to identify specific learning difficulties in advance of their occurrence. For example, the L.S.Q. has been found to be an accurate predictor of the sorts of inhibitions people will experience during a Creative Thinking course. Briefly, Reflectors are likely to find the sheer pace at which creative thinking techniques generate ideas a major problem. Theorists are inhibited by their liking for logical thinking and dislike of untidy loose ends. Pragmatists, with their dedication to things practical, suffer from difficulties in suspending judgement during the generation of ideas. Activists have the least problems with creative thinking itself but become impatient with the subsequent evaluation of the ideas generated. Predictions of learning difficulties such as these are valuable because they help to indicate what the trainer can do to alleviate or avoid the difficulties. If the difficulties are the inevitable sort that simply *have* to be worked through as an essential part of the learning process, then at least the L.S.Q. helps the trainer to hold fast through the troughs and encourage learners to do the same.

2. *Discussing the learning process*
The L.S.Q. can act as an excellent hook on which to hang a discussion about the process of learning. In our experience most training programmes begin with a declaration of the objectives and an explanation of the contents and timetable. The learning process is rarely mentioned and it is taken for granted that people will know what is involved and be able, automatically as it were, to learn from the various opportunities built into the course. How much more useful to give course members the L.S.Q. to complete and show them how to score and interpret their own results.

The following routine will suit many courses:-

● Introduce the L.S.Q. without describing the learning styles. Simply say something like: "Here we are on the brink of starting this course which is, in a sense, a concentrated learning experience. It seems that people develop different ways of learning from experience and here is a short questionnaire that should throw light on this. It only takes ten minutes or so to complete and after everyone has finished we will discuss the different styles more fully and I will show you how to score your own questionnaire".

● While they complete the questionnaire, remain on hand to answer any queries.

● As soon as people finish the L.S.Q. give them, individually, a handout with a paragraph giving a summary description of each learning style. (See Pages 10 to 15).

● When everyone has finished and read the handout, recap on the learning styles and take questions of clarification. Also explain that there are no rights or wrongs, merely different preferences. For the purposes of provoking discussion, it also helps to introduce the idea that the learning styles can be viewed as a series of steps in the total process of learning from experience:-

Step 1
The Activist tries something new or different.

Step 2
The Reflector reviews the experience.

Step 3
The Theorist accepts or rejects and integrates what has been learned from the experience.

Step 4
The Pragmatist works out when and how to apply what has been learned.

● Explain how most people have a mixture of learning styles rather than being exclusively dependent on one of the four styles (it is very rare for anyone to score zero for any style), but that, despite this, it is quite likely that one style will tend to predominate. Invite them to anticipate which style is most like them and which style is least like them.

● Give out the scoring key and get each course member to score their own L.S.Q.

● Give them the appropriate norms so that the four scores can be put in context and significant preferences identified.

● Record each person's scores on a flip chart by going round the group. Then apply the norms to highlight scores that indicate strong style preferences. There is a choice of which norms to use depending on the 'population' to which the learners belong (see Chapter 7 Pages 76 to 78). Here is an example:-

	A	R	T	P
Dick	5	(16)	(14)	13
Janet	5	(19)	(15)	(16)
Jill	(16)	9	11	(15)
Brian	9	(19)	(16)	11
Tom	(13)	12	9	(17)
etc.				

● Reflect on the scores together, drawing out conclusions for the group as a whole: "We are short of Activists and this will mean I shall have to cajole you into action from time to time"; and "The high preponderance of Pragmatists means that we must be careful to forge links between theory and practice", etc.

It takes about 45 minutes to work through these steps. They are a useful way to surface the learning process and put it in firmly and squarely on the map for the duration of the course. At intervals through the programme the L.S.Q. scores can be referred to, either to exemplify some incident that has just occurred or to pull someone's leg when they run true to form!

There are, of course, alternatives to this process. For example, the questionnaire, scoring and trainer's analyses can all be done outside a formal course session and only the results discussed in full group.

3. *Getting people to plan to expand their learning styles*
This suggestion is an extension of the last one because it presupposes that course members have completed an L.S.Q. and scored/interpreted it. Instead of leaving it at that, however, the idea is now to invite course members to analyse their responses to the questionnaire in more depth, with a view to producing some personal action plans. Probably the best way to do this is to get course members to focus on the style with the lowest score and write out a list of the relevant questionnaire items that they crossed. This procedure has been described earlier in this manual (see Page 44) so we won't repeat an illustration here. The key to success in setting people the challenge of developing a style which is not already a characteristic one for them, is undoubtedly to encourage them to set realistic, yet *specific,* personal action plans. People who want to develop the Activist style could, for example, set themselves a specific target to contribute a minimum amount at each discussion session ("I will speak for at least two unbroken minutes for every thirty minutes worth of plenary session"). People who want to develop their Reflector style could plan to volunteer to act as observers at least once per day and set themselves targets for their diligence as observers ("I will write down verbatim at least 50% of what people say"). People who want to develop their Theorist style could plan to search for the basic assumptions underpinning the various subjects being studied on the course ("I will identify and list at least five assumptions for each topic introduced on the course and verify them with the presenter"). Finally, people who want to develop their Pragmatist tendencies could plan to identify practical techniques for each subject encountered on the course ("I will identify and list at least two techniques for each course topic, describing them in 'how to do it' terms such that anyone on the course could action them correctly").

These are, of course, only examples. There are many possible action plans that could result from a careful analysis of the L.S.Q. items. Whatever plans emerge, it is useful to list them on flip charts and leave them on permanent display. This helps to act as a reminder and aids collaboration and mutual support between course members as they struggle to develop uncharacteristic behaviour patterns. If need be, time to review progress with personal action plans arising from learning styles and produce updated plans could be scheduled at the start of each day.

4. *Using L.S.Q. results to allocate roles in exercises*
Often, within the framework of an exercise on a course, trainers are able to decide which roles to distribute to which participants. Role play execises are an obvious opportunity to do this but other exercises may also lend themselves. For example, it may be appropriate to designate a leader or chairman for a team work exercise or syndicate activity. Learning style preferences can be a useful way to allocate such roles and this can be done in two different ways. When the objective is to give people roles that they are capable of carrying off convincingly, then the roles should be allocated so that they are compatible with learning style strengths. Alternatively, when the objective is to 'force' people to develop behaviours that are not already comfortably within their repertoire, the trainer can deliberately allocate roles that challenge people to overcome their learning style weaknesses. One of the authors has recently designed an exercise at the start of an interactive skills course, where course members who get high Reflector/Theorist L.S.Q. scores are put together in a group and given the following task to tackle: "Prepare to interview the trainer for 30 minutes to find out everything you need to know about this course". Meanwhile, high scoring Activists and Pragmatists are given some guidelines on how to observe, and time to prepare to do a detailed observation of the interview. All this is done quite openly with the full knowledge of everyone involved. In fact, it is important that the rationale for allocation roles is public knowledge so that people do not waste energy being suspicious of the trainer's motives.

Another example of using L.S.Q. results as the basis for allocating roles, is an exercise which has been used to help people practice the skills involved in participating in effective meetings. Six different roles are distributed in the form of objectives that each person is requested to achieve by the end of the meeting. In summary the roles are as follows:-

Objective 1
To have got your colleagues to agree a formal objective for the meeting and to have used it to review the success of the meeting.

Objective 2
To have 'chaired' the discussion effectively.

Objective 3
To have been an effective contributor of ideas.

Objective 4
To have been an effective 'devil's advocate'.

Objective 5
To have been an effective 'catalyst'.

Objective 6
To have been an effective developer of other people's ideas.

(Given the overall purpose is for someone to be given a role which will expand his style, you, the reader, might like to pause and try your hand at allocating each of the objectives to a Pragmatist, Reflector, etc.).

There are no hard and fast rules for the allocation of these roles, but more often than not they are distributed in a way that challenges each participant to go out on a limb and experiment with ways of behaving that do not come 'naturally'. In this case the objectives are allocated on the following basis:-

Objective 1
To an Activist.

Objective 2
To a Reflector or Activist.

Objective 3
To a Reflector.

Objective 4
To a Pragmatist or Activist.

Objective 5
To a Theorist.

Objective 6
To a Theorist or Pragmatist.

5. *Using L.S.Q. results to constitute groups, teams or syndicates*
Much has been written about methodologies for putting together individuals who can blend their different strengths to form a coherent team. The L.S.Q. offers another basis for mixing groups in a training situation.

Perhaps the most obvious way to use learning styles as a basis for putting groups on courses together, is to ensure that all groups are matched and that the full range of learning styles are available to each group. Suppose, for example, there were 12 people together on a course and they were to be split into two syndicates with six members in each. The L.S.Q. scores for the total course are as follows:-

	A	R	T	P
Mike	6	(19)	(16)	12
Cathie	6	(16)	(15)	10
John	(12)	7	8	(17)
Peter	(13)	12	10	5
David	9	12	12	13
Bill	(14)	11	8	10
Sheila	(18)	10	8	13
Ian	10	(17)	(16)	(18)
Anita	9	7	(15)	(17)
Malcolm	(15)	6	7	7
Ruth	(16)	8	6	(16)
George	7	(17)	(15)	(18)

Circles indicate a strong style preference when the General Norms on Page 75 are applied to these scores.

Given these scores, the best way to match two syndicates would be as follows:-

Syndicate 1	Syndicate 2
Sheila (A)	Bill (A)
Peter (A)	Malcolm (A)
John (A/P)	Ruth (A/P)
Ian (R/T/P)	George (R/T/P)
Mike (R/T)	Cathie (R/T)
Anita (T/P)	David (average all rounder with no strong preferences)

One of the authors has conducted experiments where the performance of syndicates constituted at random have been compared with the performance of syndicates constituted on the basis of learning styles. The performance of syndicates with a full range of learning styles available to it has always been found to be superior. They are better at achieving set objectives, produce higher quality work, meet deadlines more comfortably and interact more efficiently with less interrupting, more listening, more building, etc., etc. Success is still further enhanced if the learning styles of each syndicate member are made public. This seems to help syndicates to identify the relative strengths and weaknesses of its members and allocate roles in such a way that strengths are fully exploited.

Of course there may be good reasons for deliberately constituting groups on an entirely different basis. For example, it may be desirable to put all the Activist/Pragmatists together in one syndicate and all the Reflector/Theorists together in another. This is a mixing technique which helps to create conditions where characteristically high contributors are somewhat curtailed and where low contributors have a chance to flower in an environment where their more dominant colleagues have been removed.

Using Learning Styles After a Training Programme
We conclude this chapter giving ideas to the trainer on how to use the L.S.Q. by looking at the implications of learning styles for follow-up activities.

1. *Producing plans to implement what has been learned*
   Actually we cannot talk about follow-up activities without considering the possibility of concluding an off-the-job course with some 'bridge building' to help people survive the perils of transferring what has been learned on the course to the very different circumstances of the on-the-job situation. Many courses conclude with an action planning phase where people are invited to take stock of what they have learned, the working situation they are about to return to (warts and all), and the likely hazards in continuing to develop new found skills or apply new knowledge. Obviously a person's learning style preference should be taken into account in reaching feasible action plans. Also we suggest that the learning style of the person's boss should also loom large in any end-of-course planning. The lists in the previous chapter (Page 55), spelling out the different types of support that are likely to emerge from bosses with different learning styles, are particularly pertinent here. They can be reproduced as useful handouts for course members to refer to as they produce their action plans. Incidentally, if course members are paired off to help each other produce action plans then Pragmatists are invaluable and should never be paired together. It is much more useful to spread people with Pragmatist tendencies around so

that they can use their skills to help tether Activists, Reflectors and Theorists to reality when it comes to producing action plans that are really feasible.

2. *Getting course members to check out the learning styles of bosses, subordinates and colleagues*
   Provided course members have been shown the ropes adequately when it comes to administering the L.S.Q., scoring it, and applying appropriate norms to the results, we see no objection to encouraging them to give the L.S.Q. to people who are likely to have an impact on their day-to-day learning. Bosses are obviously key figures in this regard but subordinates and colleagues are also likely candidates. If course members are reticent about administering the L.S.Q. themselves, without any 'expert' help, then the trainer can offer to come and do it as part of the 'after-sales service' following a training course of some kind. Besides being helpful in its own right, such an L.S.Q. session with a real work team can act as an effective entree for the trainer – especially if he/she is adept at interpreting the L.S.Q. and counselling interested parties in its implications.

3. *Running follow-up clinics*
   L.S.Q. results should always be kept for future reference and are especially useful if it is planned to hold follow-up clinics at some interval after the initial training. One of the authors has held many such one-day clinics offering them, on an entirely voluntary basis, four to eight months after attendance on the initial training programme. Where numbers and administrative arrangements permit, it has been found that the clinic is enhanced if Activists, Reflectors, Theorists and Pragmatists attend in more or less equal numbers. This is because the learning styles have a significant effect on the problems of application people are likely to have encountered in the period since they attended the course. Any review of the successes people have notched up, and the difficulties they have encountered, is enriched by having a broad spectrum of learning styles present. To some extent they counter-balance one another in a way that can be mutually supportive and stimulate fresh efforts to overcome transfer problems.

   Follow-up clinics are also a golden opportunity to re-administer the L.S.Q. to see if there have been any significant changes as a result of the training and subsequent back at work experiences. If the training had been aimed at helping people to become all-round learners, it is clearly important to see if the L.S.Q. re-test results confirm this tendency. In these circumstances the L.S.Q. acts as one means of validating the success of the training in achieving this objective.

How to Use the L.S.Q. to Aid Adviser/Learner Compatibility
We have referred several times to the illumination the L.S.Q. should offer to an individual. The self knowledge acquired by the trainer from his own L.S.Q. is a special case. It not only tells him something about his own approach to learning but also should tell him something about the ways in which he is likely to be most comfortable in helping the learning of others. The Activist trainer will tend to jolly people along and assume a preparedness to go at risk which may not be there. The Reflector trainer will tend to emphasise observation and painstaking reviews. Theorist trainers will tend towards prescriptive models and structure. Pragmatist trainers will be at pains to establish high face validity through the demonstration of practical applications.

Fascinatingly, the evidence we have at present indicates that trainers tend to have high Activist tendencies. A comparison of mean scores for seven occupational groups puts trainers ($N = 96$) in the following positions in the league table:-

Activist	2nd	(second only to Salesmen)
Reflector	5th	(only Production Managers and Salesmen are lower)
Theorist	6th	(Salesmen are equally low)
Pragmatist	7th	(no-one is lower)

We obviously need data for a larger population of trainers, but at present, this confirms the view that the trainer is often an exhibitionist on some sort of ego-trip! Perhaps this is why so many trainers (one of the authors includes himself in this category) are so enthusiastic about learning by doing and have little time for other alternatives.

While we do not yet have direct evidence from the L.S.Q., evidence from complementary research by Margerison and by Hofstede shows that there is often a difference in preferred learning styles, at least in Business Schools, between faculty and learners. We believe the L.S.Q. should be used by all trainers to assess possible differences between themselves and those they are helping to learn. They then have the option of either trying to increase their own range of learning styles, or of deliberately building in activities not normally congruent with their own style in an attempt to meet the needs of the learner.

Learning Styles and Learning to Learn
On pages 64 to 66 we give ideas on how to use L.S.Q. results to create a discussion on learning. Such a discussion can be enhanced, and action encouraged, by giving people 'Using Your Learning Styles' as an action work

book. The major issue of learning to learn has been analysed, and appropriate actions identified by Alan Mumford in his monograph 'Learning to Learn for Managers' (see reading list on page 83). The monograph covers a range of issues and processes, including points about the strategy and problems involved.

Conclusion

We hope this chapter has given trainers a number of ideas on how the L.S.Q. can be used to enhance training activities. Clearly there are numerous other possible applications in the broad fields of selection and training. To our knowledge the L.S.Q. has already been used:-

● To select salesmen for the computer industry.

● To select graduate management trainees.

● To put together compatible project teams.

● To screen line managers being trained as observers at assessment centres.

● To aid career counselling and guidance.

● As part of an in-company annual appraisal system.

● As part of a market research survey.

As the number of people using the L.S.Q. grows, we hope it will prove useful in still more ways. We also hope that you will want to assist in developing the use of the L.S.Q. by participating in the 'L.S.Q. Club', details of which are given in Chapter 7 on Page 82.

This chapter contains the statistics compiled from the version of the L.S.Q. available before the revised edition. The revised edition has been tested to see whether the results differ significantly from the original edition. There are no statistically significant differences. We have therefore included the pre 1986 norms. Members of the L.S.Q. Club, which you are invited to join (see page 82 for details), have contributed to the compilation of norms for different occupational groups.

Reliability
The consistency, or reliability, of the L.S.Q. has been checked by getting a total of 50 people to complete the questionnaire twice, with a two week gap between the two occasions. The correlation (Pearson's product-moment coefficient of correlation) between the two sets of results was a very satisfactory 0.89. People with strong Theorist and Reflector preferences were the *most* consistent with correlations of 0.95 and 0.92 respectively. Pragmatists produced a test-retest consistency of 0.87, and Activists were the least consistent with a correlation of 0.81.

Validity
The validity of a questionnaire such as the L.S.Q. is harder to determine especially in the area where there are few established questionnaires to draw comparisons with. (Correlations with the Kolb and Fry L.S.I. are given later in this chapter). One of the authors has checked its validity on courses by making specific behavioural predictions (such as those listed on Page 63) based solely on the L.S.Q. results. The predictions have been found to be largely accurate but this hardly constitutes a respectable proof of validity. *Face* validity (as opposed to *real* validity) for the L.S.Q. is not in doubt. It has been rare for us to encounter anyone who disputes the accuracy of their L.S.Q. result. When this has occurred, it usually stemmed from a misunderstanding about the styles and was resolved after further explanation. More objective data on the validity of the L.S.Q. will no doubt become available – especially through the formation of an L.S.Q. Club (see Page 82).

The Amount of Overlap Between the Four Learning Styles
The correlations are:-

	Activist	Reflector	Theorist	Pragmatist
Activist	X	-0.013	0.097	0.299
Reflector	-0.013	X	0.71	0.42
Theorist	0.097	0.71	X	0.54
Pragmatist	0.299	0.42	0.54	X

This means that in descending order of likelihood, the most common combinations are:-

1st   Reflector/Theorist
2nd   Theorist/Pragmatist
3rd   Reflector/Pragmatist
4th   Activist/Pragmatist

The other two combinations (Activist/Reflector and Activist/Theorist) are less likely to occur since in both cases the correlation between them is virtually zero.

Norms
In all groups A represents the top 10%; B the next 20%; C the middle 40%; D the next 20%; E the bottom 10%. All norms have been rounded to the nearest whole number.

General Norms for a Wide Cross Section of Managerial/Professional People working in U.K. Industry.
N = 1302

	Activist	Reflector	Theorist	Pragmatist
A	13-20	18-20	16-20	17-20
B	11-12	15-17	14-15	15-16
C	7-10	12-14	11-13	12-14
D	4-6	9-11	8-10	9-11
E	0-3	0-8	0-7	0-8
	Mean 9.3	Mean 13.6	Mean 12.5	Mean 13.7
	SD 2.9	SD 3.1	SD 3.2	SD 2.9

There now follow norms for seven different occupational groups.

Salesmen N = 89

	Activist	Reflector	Theorist	Pragmatist
A	17-20	15-20	17-20	18-20
B	15-16	12-14	14-16	16-17
C	12-14	10-11	9-13	13-15
D	9-11	7-9	6-8	10-12
E	0-8	0-6	0-5	0-9
	Mean 13.3	Mean 11.5	Mean 11.4	Mean 14.1
	SD 2.9	SD 2.8	SD 3.6	SD 3.0

Trainers N = 96

	Activist	Reflector	Theorist	Pragmatist
A	16-20	17-20	17-20	17-20
B	14-15	15-16	14-16	15-16
C	9-13	11-14	9-13	12-14
D	6-8	8-10	6-8	8-11
E	0-5	0-7	0-5	0-7
	Mean 11.2	Mean 12.9	Mean 11.4	Mean 12.4
	SD 3.8	SD 3.7	SD 3.6	SD 3.1

Marketing Managers N = 93

	Activist	Reflector	Theorist	Pragmatist
A	13-20	18-20	16-20	17-20
B	11-12	16-17	14-15	15-16
C	7-10	12-15	10-13	13-14
D	4-6	9-11	7-9	10-12
E	0-3	0-8	0-6	0-9
	Mean 9.3	Mean 13.8	Mean 12.5	Mean 13.6
	SD 2.9	SD 3.2	SD 3.4	SD 2.4

Engineering/Science Graduates N = 73

	Activist	Reflector	Theorist	Pragmatist
A	13-20	18-20	16-20	16-20
B	11-12	16-17	14-15	14-15
C	6-10	12-15	11-13	11-13
D	4-5	9-11	8-10	9-10
E	0-3	0-8	0-7	0-8
	Mean 8.6	Mean 14.2	Mean 12.2	Mean 12.7
	SD 3.8	SD 3.6	SD 3.2	SD 3.0

Research and Development Managers N = 262

	Activist	Reflector	Theorist	Pragmatist
A	13-20	18-20	17-20	17-20
B	10-12	16-17	15-16	15-16
C	6-9	13-15	12-14	12-14
D	4-5	10-12	9-11	9-11
E	0-3	0-9	0-8	0-8
	Mean 8.0	Mean 14.5	Mean 13.1	Mean 13.4
	SD 3.4	SD 3.0	SD 2.8	SD 2.8

Production Managers N = 78

	Activist	Reflector	Theorist	Pragmatist
A	12-20	17-20	19-20	19-20
B	9-11	15-16	17-18	17-18
C	6-8	11-14	14-16	15-16
D	3-5	7-10	12-13	12-14
E	0-2	0-6	0-11	0-11
	Mean 7.4	Mean 12.7	Mean 15.2	Mean 16.0
	SD 3.4	SD 4.0	SD 1.3	SD 1.9

Finance Managers N = 60

	Activist	Reflector	Theorist	Pragmatist
A	10-20	19-20	18-20	18-20
B	8-9	16-18	16-17	16-17
C	6-7	14-15	13-15	14-15
D	3-5	10-13	11-12	11-13
E	0-2	0-9	0-10	0-10
	Mean 7.0	Mean 14.9	Mean 14.5	Mean 15.3
	SD 1.7	SD 1.6	SD 2.2	SD 1.4

Dominant Styles

We have done a sampling exercise to find the extent to which managers are dominated by one style, instead of being all round learners. The results sustain our basic proposition; that learners often have a strong preference for one learning style. Strong is defined as groups A and B in our norms. i.e. the top 30% of scores.

Random sample of 300 managers

With one strong preference	35%
With two strong preferences	24%
With three strong preferences	20%
With four strong preferences	2%
With no stong preference	19%

National Norms

To date we have only limited information about the effects of national differences on L.S.Q. norms. Norms for 126 Middle managers in the U.K. very closely match the General norms given on Page 75. We have given the L.S.Q. to small groups of 42 American and 46 Canadian managers and this is obviously too small a sample to allow any difinitive conclusions to be drawn from the results. Comparing the mean scores for the three groups we have:-

	Activist	Reflector	Theorist	Pragmatist
British Managers	8.7	12.9	13.5	14.5
Canadian Managers	8.5	13.9	13.6	14.0
American Managers	9.5	12.0	14.5	14.5

Male and Female Norms

Our data is also limited when it comes to drawing conclusions about differences between men and women. We have data based on 174 female managers. The norms are as follows:-

Female British Managers N = 174

	Activist	Reflector	Theorist	Pragmatist
A	16-20	19-20	17-20	18-20
B	13-15	16-18	14-16	15-17
C	8-12	12-15	11-13	12-14
D	6-7	7-11	8-10	7-11
E	0-5	0-6	0-7	0-6
	Mean 10.3	Mean 13.4	Mean 12.7	Mean 12.6
	SD 3.8	SD 3.3	SD 3.6	SD 2.9

These results indicate that, in comparison with their male counterparts, female managers are higher Activists (perhaps they had to be!) and lower Pragmatists.

The Significance of L.S.Q. Items Ticked and Crossed

We have analysed a random sample of 100 completed questionnaires to discover ticking and crossing patterns. As the results below show, a few items in the current version of the L.S.Q. are ticked by 90% or more people. Obviously these items are failing to discriminate adequately and could therefore be excluded. We would, however, prefer to retain them until more data is available, when it may be possible to reduce the number of items in future versions of the L.S.Q.

Activist		Reflector		Theorist		Pragmatist	
L.S.Q. item	% who ticked	L.S.Q. item	% who ticked	L.S.Q. item	% who ticked	L.S.Q. item	% who ticked
2	36	7	48	1	82	5	68
4	52	13	79	3	88	9	95
6	55	15	81	8	80	11	72
10	76	16	85	12	44	19	86
17	29	25	33	14	63	21	86
23	94	28	76	18	83	27	84
24	84	29	68	20	87	35	56
32	64	31	67	22	19	37	86
34	42	33	70	26	34	44	90
38	15	36	33	30	61	49	79
40	37	39	55	42	55	50	95
43	30	41	67	47	89	53	85
45	19	46	75	51	87	54	83
48	28	52	85	57	92	56	93
58	29	55	44	61	54	59	77
64	50	60	67	63	92	65	31
71	19	62	48	68	72	69	60
72	15	66	91	75	75	70	37
74	36	67	56	77	78	73	67
79	80	76	89	78	44	80	30

Summing the four scores for Activist, Reflector, Theorist and Pragmatist we have found that the lowest combined score so far encountered is 22 and the highest 59 with a mean, for the whole population tested so far, of 48.6 and standard deviation of 8.2. We were naturally curious to see if a high or low combined score was particularly associated with any of the learning styles. In fact there are some very significant trends. The correlations between style preference and high or low combined scores is as follows:-

Theorist   0.90
Reflector   0.80
Pragmatist   0.74
Activist   0.48

These correlations indicate a particularly strong association between the Theorist style and the tendency to be a high or low ticker of the questionnaire items. In other words, a person with a strong Theorist style is likely to have a high combined score (i.e. ticked lots of items) and conversely, a person with a low Theorist style is likely to have a low combined score (i.e. crossed lots of items).

Correlation Between the L.S.Q. and the L.S.I.
We know of two relatively small samples of managers who have completed both the L.S.Q. and the (pre 1985) Kolb Learning Styles Inventory (L.S.I.). In both samples there were dramatic differences of scores on apparently similar styles. In our view this is not surprising, given the significant difference in descriptions and in type of questions. Kolb has now published a revised version of the L.S.I., and we know of no comparisons of results with this version.

The L.S.Q. Club
We have formed an L.S.Q. club which collects and shares information. The idea is to help develop further both the data about learning styles and the ideas and information about the use of L.S.Q. and learning activities. We want both to acquire more information for our own purposes and to assist with the circulation of that information to other users of L.S.Q.

Membership is open to anyone who uses the L.S.Q. and who is prepared to give information and wants to receive it.

You give

● Information about L.S.Q. results, on a predetermined format covering age, function, nationality, sex.

● Information about your use of learning styles/L.S.Q./learning activities.

You Receive

● Regular, probably annual, updating of norms (including new groups).

● Summaries of developments by Honey, Mumford and other users.

You join the L.S.Q. Club by writing to Peter Honey at 10 Linden Avenue, Maidenhead, Berkshire, asking for further details.

Further Reading
As this is a working manual we have not followed academic conventions about footnotes, but the following notes will help those who want to follow up some of the sources mentioned.

1. Kolb's *"Learning Cycle and Learning Style Inventory"*. See D.A. Kolb Experiential Learning, Prentice Hall 1984.

2. Learning Styles of Teachers and Learners.
See C. Margerison and R. Lewis *"Management Educators and Their Clients"*, in Advances in Management Education, Edited by J. Beck and T. Cox; Wiley 1981. Also G. Hofstede *"Businessmen and Business School Faculty"*, Journal of Management Studies, 15, No. 1, 1978.

3. For Teaching Methods.
D. Binstead *"Design for Learning"* in Journal of European Industrial Training (Vol. 4, No. 8, 1980).

4. For Learning Opportunities, especially on the job.
A.C. Mumford *"Making Experience Pay"*, McGraw Hill, 1980.

5. For Action Learning.
R.W. Revans *"Action Learning and Development of Self"*, in Management Self Development, Ed. T. Boydell and M. Pedlar, Gower, 1981. D. Casey and D. Pearce *"More Than Management Development"*, Gower, 1981.

6. General Model of Development.
Bert Juch *"Personal Development"*, Wiley, 1983.

7. For Learning to Learn.
A.C. Mumford *"Learning to Learn for Managers"* Journal of European Industrial Training Vol. 10 No. 2 1986.

8. Learning Styles Articles
Peter Honey *"Learning Styles and Self Development"* Training and Development Jan. 1984. Peter Honey *"Learning Styles - their relevence to Training Courses"* Training Officer April 1983. Roy Canning *"Management Self-Development"* Richard Striven *"Learning Cycles"* Both in Journal of European Industrial Training Vol. 8 No. 1 Ian Hinton *"Learning to Manage and Managing to Learn"* Industrial & Commercial Training Vol. 16 No.3 Alan Mumford *"Learning at Home"* Programmed Learning and Education Technology Vol. 22 No. 4.Leslie Rae *"The Application of Learning Styles"* Industrial and Commercial Training Vol. 18 No. 2.

Notes on the 1986 Edition of the Manual and L.S.Q.

Since the original Manual and L.S.Q. was published in 1982 it has been used in the UK, USA, Sweden, Switzerland, France, South Africa, New Zealand, Australia, Malaysia and Hong Kong to mention but a few. The L.S.Q. has also been translated into many different languages. We have reviewed our own experience, and that of members of the L.S.Q. Club, in producing the revised edition of the L.S.Q. included with this Manual.

A shorter version of the L.S.Q. could be produced, eliminating some of the non-discriminating items which we identify on page 80. One experiment with a 40 item questionnaire produced statistically the same results. However, we believe that the time saved to complete the questionnaire is not a significant factor, and that the more extensive list of questions is more helpful in generating discussion about specific behaviours. For many purposes the actual scores achieved are less important than the review of the questions.

This revised 1986 L.S.Q. is 'improved' deliberately in only one respect. We have taken out the English slang or colloquialisms which made the L.S.Q. less understandable to managers outside the UK. We have made no other alterations in order to sustain the connection with our original material, now so widely used.

We have run the 1986 edition in parallel with the earlier one and found no significant differences in the results. We can confirm, therefore, that the norms based on the 1982 edition are equally valid for the new edition.